The Gospel in Numbers

Independently Published

Copyright © 2022

All rights reserved.

ISBN: 9798401274014

The Gospel in Numbers

Walking with Christ in the Wilderness of Life

TABLE OF CONTENTS

INTRODUCTION

This book comes as result of God's goodness to me. After four decades of seeking to proclaim the truths of the Bible, I am continually blown away by the profound way in which a voluminous work, containing 66 books from dozens of writers spread across centuries of time, can have one theme and one great Hero!

Jesus is the key to understanding the Word of God, for He is fully revealed in both Old and New Testaments. So, why write a book about the gospel in Numbers, you ask? The answer to this question is found in looking back and looking forward. Please allow me to offer both an explanation and an introduction.

My name is Tony Collins. I am a most ordinary pastor and a most fortunate husband, father, and "G-Dad." Mine has been a journey of God's saving grace and mercy. I was born in the early 1960's, and my childhood years were spent in a home with my mother and grandmother. My parents divorced when I was just a baby. My dad moved to northern Indiana where he went to work in the steel mills. My mom moved into the trailer with my grandmother, and that is where I spent the next thirteen years.

I was blessed with two wonderful grandmothers who loved and provided for me during my early years. At the age of nine, I heard the good news of the Gospel and trusted Christ as my Savior. My life radically changed, as did the lives of my mom and grandmother. God used my conversion as the catalyst to bring the whole family into a right relationship with the Lord. I got baptized, and we all went to church together.

When I was thirteen, my mom married a man named Ed, and I got a stepdad. Ed became the greatest male role model I had ever known. He loved the Lord, and he loved me and my mom. We were so blessed. We attended West Broadway Baptist Church in Lenoir City, Tennessee, where I announced my call to preach and was later ordained to the Gospel ministry.

In these past four decades, the Lord has blessed me with an amazing wife (Janey – the perfect pastor's wife with hugs and love for everybody), two awesome sons (Justen and Eric), two beautiful daughters-in-law (Samantha and Dakota), and four wonderful grandchildren (Oz, Trooper, Stu, and Layla).

God has blessed me with the opportunity of preparing for ministry by pursuing and furthering my education. I was able to attend Liberty University (B.S.) and the Southern Baptist Theological Seminary (M. Div.), along with post-graduate studies through Trinity Seminary and finally received a Doctorate Degree (D. Div.) from Toronto Baptist Seminary. During these many years, I have served as the lead pastor of three Southern Baptist Churches across eastern Tennessee.

I would like to acknowledge several people that have greatly aided in the realization of this book. My wife and my son Justen have proofread and edited, along with Jenni Hayes – a dear friend and secretary at BBC. I would also like to thank two of our associate pastors (they will be introduced at the beginning of their chapters) who each contributed passages from sermons that they preached during our study. Lastly, I thank the wonderful, gracious people of Broadway Baptist Church who attended and listened to these messages.

Having grown up in a Baptist church myself, I learned Bible stories as a child. I was taught these stories and came away amazed by the great men and women of the Bible. However, these stories were taught to me primarily as moralistic anecdotes. I was encouraged to have faith like Abraham, to be strong like Samson, to be courageous like David when he slew Goliath, or to pray like Daniel.

While it is true that these stories can teach us by way of example, they really come to greater usefulness when we view them through the lens of the Gospel. I did not realize growing up that Jesus is the fulfillment of all these Old Testament stories, and that He alone was always faithful and true.

As we learn from studying the Old Testament, each of the great Bible heroes and heroines had their own weaknesses, flaws, and sinfulness. None of them were able to achieve "full" faithfulness – always, forever, and until the end! Only Christ is the perfect One, yet God penned down these stories to reveal in type and foreshadow what the coming Messiah would be like. A type, or shadow, cannot fully display the glory of the object it represents, but it can help us more clearly see things about the object it represents, especially once the object is fully revealed. The Old Testament is God's progressive unveiling of the Divine object – the long-awaited Messiah, Jesus!

This is clear when we consider how Jesus spent his first afternoon on that resurrection day. According to Luke 24, Jesus walked with two disciples on the road to Emmaus that day. He could have appeared to the masses, yet He chose two downhearted men walking from Jerusalem. Listen to their conversation as recounted by Luke:

"That very day two of them were going to a village named Emmaus, about seven miles from Jerusalem, and they were talking with each other about all these things that had happened. While they were talking and discussing together, Jesus himself drew near and went with them. But their eyes were kept from recognizing him. And he said to them, 'What is this conversation that you are holding with each other as you walk?' And they stood still, looking sad. Then one of them, named Cleopas, answered him, 'Are you the only visitor to Jerusalem who does not know the things that have happened there in these days?' And he said to them, 'What things?' And they said to him, 'Concerning Jesus of Nazareth, a man who was a prophet mighty in deed and word before God and all the people, and how our chief priests and rulers delivered him up to be condemned to death and crucified him. But we had hoped that he was the one to redeem Israel. Yes, and besides all this, it is now the third day since these things happened. Moreover, some women of our company amazed us. They were at the tomb early in the morning, and when they did not find his body, they came back saying that they had even seen a vision of angels, who said that he was alive. Some of those who were with us went to the tomb and found it just as the women had said, but him they did not see.' To this Jesus replied, 'O foolish ones, and slow of heart to believe all that the prophets have spoken! Was it not necessary that the Christ should suffer these things and enter into his glory?' And beginning with Moses and all the Prophets, he interpreted to them in all the Scriptures the things concerning himself."

Later in the Upper Room, Jesus would expound the Scriptures to His disciples. Luke records it as follows, "Then he said to them, 'These are my words that I spoke to you while I was still with you, that everything written about me in the Law of Moses and the Prophets, and the Psalms must be fulfilled.' Then he opened their minds to understand the Scriptures, and said to them, 'Thus it is written, that the Christ should suffer and on the third day rise from the dead, and that repentance for the forgiveness of sins should be proclaimed in his name to all nations, beginning from Jerusalem.'"

Jesus gave them a paradigm shift by viewing the Old Testament Scriptures through the lens of the cross! In other words, he was helping them put on their "Jesus glasses." Once we realize that the Old Testament serves to illustrate in vivid color the coming of Christ, we see Him on every page and in every event. We see a big God working His eternal redemption plan!

One of my goals in writing this book is to help others put on their "Jesus" glasses – to see Him more clearly and to love Him more dearly. The meditations found in this book were compiled from a series of sermons on the Old Testament book of Numbers that were preached from the pulpit of Broadway Baptist Church in Maryville, Tennessee. It is my sincere hope that these thoughts and reflections upon the Gospel as found in the great Exodus narrative might stir your heart to love the Lord and increase your desire to walk with Him each day. It was not my goal to write an academic commentary on these Scriptures, for I am quite confident that there exists a vast supply of scholarly, critical works that meet the need for academic pursuit.

My desire is to enable the average Christian (the "layperson," if you will) to enjoy the glories of the Christ revealed within the sacred text of Scripture. Therefore, this endeavor will not include footnotes, technical jargon, or very much of the original languages. It is aimed to be read more as devotional reading than academic pursuit. It is simply the message of the gospel as shared by an ordinary pastor.

If you recall, I said the answer to the question of why I would choose to write this particular book was twofold, and the second motivation has to do with looking forward. As I look at the evangelical landscape around me, I see many who are advocating (to use their own term) "unhitching from the Old Testament." Allow me to be clear as to my stance – I believe we are people of a whole book!

It is impossible to clearly understand the New Testament without the foundation of the Old Testament. Not only is the New Testament a fulfillment of the Old, but the Old Testament gives foundation to the New Testament, while also painting a glorious picture of Christ. There is much we would never fully know or enjoy about Christ coming into the world without the Old Testament Scripture.

The beauties of our Christ are fully revealed, foreshadowed, and found throughout the whole Word of God. To "unhitch" from the first 39 books of the Bible is to lose our foundation and much of the glory revealed in Christ. Rather than "unhitching," let us eagerly put on our Jesus glasses and see clearly those very glories revealed in our most wonderful Savior!

I pray that this book helps you see that God has been actively engaged in redeeming a people for Himself since the beginning of time. The Old Testament reveals a Sovereign God working throughout human history to redeem and restore all that was lost in the garden by Adam.

Rejoice! The second Adam (Christ) restores all that the first Adam forfeited through disobedience. May God open our eyes to see Him clearly and love Him dearly. He and He alone is worthy.

Soli Deo Gloria,
Tony

THE FAITHFULNESS OF GOD

Written for our instruction, the Bible stories that we grew up with were recorded for our learning. These are not simply moralistic stories teaching us moral lessons. Yes, they can teach those lessons, but more importantly, they teach us the ways of God. The Lord is the centerpiece of all Scripture.

1 Corinthians 10:1-12, "For I do not want you to be unaware, brothers, that our fathers were all under the cloud, and all passed through the sea, and all were baptized into Moses in the cloud and in the sea, and all ate the same spiritual food, and all drank the same spiritual drink. For they drank from the spiritual Rock that followed them, and the Rock was Christ. Nevertheless, with most of them God was not pleased, for they were overthrown in the wilderness. Now these things took place as examples for us, that we might not desire evil as they did. Do not be idolaters as some of them were; as it is written, 'The people sat down to eat and drink and rose up to play.' We must not indulge in sexual immorality as some of them did, and twenty-three thousand fell in a single day. We must not put Christ to the test, as some of them did and were destroyed by serpents, nor grumble, as some of them did and were destroyed by the Destroyer. Now these things happened to them as an example, but they were written down for our instruction, on whom the end of the ages has come. Therefore, let anyone who thinks that he stands take heed lest he fall." (ESV, all Scripture references will be the ESV unless indicated otherwise)

There is a philosophy that is gaining ground – even in evangelical circles. It is the notion that as New Testament Christians we need to disconnect from the Old Testament Scriptures. The word used by some prominent pastors is "unhitch." They advocate that we need to distance ourselves from the very Old Testament that Jesus himself read, quoted, and fulfilled. If we cut out the first 39 books of the Bible, we have literally ripped the heart out of the New Testament as well.

It is impossible for us to clearly understand what Paul is talking about in 1 Corinthians 10 if we have no knowledge of the exodus and the wilderness wanderings of the children of Israel. We would have no clue who these people are, much less what Paul is talking about. But as we see in that passage in 1 Corinthians, Paul repeatedly says that these things were written for our instruction, and he said, "do not be like them." He said, "I do not want you to be unaware" of what has happened in the past and do not be like them.

Do not be like the idolaters who sat down to eat and drink and rose up to play. Do not be like them. Do not be like those that went lusting after the things of Egypt. Do not be like them. Do not be like those that rebelled and were of unbelief. Do not be like those who were the grumblers and the complainers as some of them were.

We have much to learn from the book of Numbers. We have the whole Bible, and this whole Bible is one grand narrative. It is one glorious story of God's redeeming work. How wonderful to be able to have the whole story!

Numbers 1:1-4, "The LORD spoke to Moses in the wilderness of Sinai, in the tent of meeting, on the first day of the second month, in the second year after they had come out of the land of Egypt, saying, 'Take a census of all the congregation of the people of Israel, by clans, by fathers' houses, according to the number of names, every male, head by head. From twenty years old and upward, all in Israel who are able to go to war, you and Aaron shall list them, company by company. And there shall be with you a man from each tribe, each man being the head of the house of his fathers.'"

The subject of the promised land – Canaan Land – is a subject that has been written about quite a lot. There are many songs that we grew up singing that come from the thought of the promised land, Canaan Land. Now, many of these songs are good songs, but perhaps they are not the best interpretation of the story.

Often these hymns indicate that the promised land is heaven, and crossing the Jordan is death, and the other side of the Jordan is the promised land. In these songs, the promised land is a picture of heaven. Now, the reality is that the promised land is not at all a picture of heaven, for when they got into the promised land, that is where the battle started. That is where the war took place.

I think a better analogy is that the promised land is a picture of the victorious Christian life, a life being lived in obedience rather than in disobedience. It is a life being lived in accordance with the will of God, not in rejection of the will of God as was true of the wilderness generation.

Theology is often taught more through the songs we sing than the sermons we preach, such as "On Jordan's Stormy Banks, I Stand."

"On Jordan's stormy banks I stand,
And cast a wishful eye
To Canaan's fair and happy land,
Where my possessions lie.

I am bound for the promised land,
I am bound for the promised land;
Oh, who will come and go with me?
I am bound for the promised land."

Or how about this oldie I remember hearing as a young
boy? "Canaan Land Is Just in Sight"

"Moses led God's children forty years he led them,
Through the cold and through the night;
Tho' they said, 'Let's turn back,' Moses said, 'Keep goin',
Canaan land is just in sight.'

And there will be no sorrow there in that tomorrow,
We will be there by and by;
Milk and honey flowing there is where I'm going,
Canaan land is just in sight.

Now though we walk thru valleys, 'Tho' we climb high
mountains,
We can not give up the fight;
We must be like Moses, we must keep on going;
Canaan land is just in sight.

And there will be no sorrow there in that tomorrow,
We will be there by and by;
Milk and honey flowing there is where I'm going,
Canaan land is just in sight."

I suggest that a more fitting hymn to accompany our
study in the book of Numbers would be the hymn "Trust
and Obey."

"When we walk with the Lord in the light of His Word,
What a glory He sheds on our way!
While we do His good will, He abides with us still,
And with all who will trust and obey.

Trust and obey, for there's no other way
To be happy in Jesus, but to trust and obey."

As we think about the book of Numbers, we need to remember that it is a part of a five-book collection called the Pentateuch. The five books of Moses form together one volume. The book of Numbers does not exist in isolation, but it is a continuation of the Exodus story which began in Genesis. In Genesis, God makes a covenant with Abraham and his descendants to give them the land as an inheritance. In Exodus, God remembers the covenant (not in the sense that he had forgotten the way humans do) and redeems his people from the bondage of slavery in Egypt.

Next comes the book of Leviticus, where God is demonstrating and revealing His holiness. The book of Leviticus, perhaps more than any other book in the Old Testament, puts the spotlight upon the holiness of God. And then we come to the book of Numbers.

As we found in the opening verse, the Book of Numbers takes us back to the setting of the closing of the Book of Exodus. The children of Israel are still at Mount Sinai. They are encamped at Mount Sinai and will remain there through the first ten chapters of the Book of Numbers. It is a continuation of the story of the redeemed people of God.

If I had to choose a theme for all of our study in the book of Numbers, it would be this: "The faithfulness of God and the unfaithfulness of man."

In our study of Numbers, we are going to find that there are two generations. There is the generation of unbelief that wander in the wilderness and never see the promised land, and then there is the next generation, the generation of faith that claims the promised land.

It is their journeys that form the story. A journey of unbelief marked by frustration is followed by a journey of faith that ends in victory. Ours is a story of a journey as well, and often mine has included both the frustration of unbelief and the victory claimed by faith.

Journeys do not always go as planned! My wife and I experienced this some years ago. Around noon one day, Janey and I left from McGhee Tyson Airport in Maryville, Tennessee on our way to Dallas, Texas where we were to change planes and fly to Vancouver, Canada. There we would spend a restful evening and morning before boarding a cruise ship to Alaska. Those were our journey plans.

Now, as we boarded the plane, the weather map in the terminal showed all clear skies across the whole country – except for one tiny storm cell. There should be smooth sailing all the way to Vancouver. That was encouraging.

About an hour and a half into our flight, the pilot came on and said that he had been informed that there was some bad weather in the Dallas area and he would keep us posted. Now, I was not sure what this weather was or how concerning that it might be, but in about another thirty or forty-five minutes, he came back on the intercom and said he had been advised that we were to be in a holding pattern.

We were, in other words, going to be circling around up in the air, waiting for the weather to clear in Dallas, and so we circled and circled and circled some more. In a little while, he came back on the speaker and said he had been instructed that we were going to be rerouted and we were going to Oklahoma City. Now, Oklahoma City is a nice place, I am sure, but it was not on our itinerary. It was not somewhere that we were supposed to be going.

Alas, we made our little trip over to Oklahoma City, and landed there along with a lot of other planes that had been rerouted. We sat on the tarmac there for about three hours until finally he said that we had clearance and we were going to be taking off and making our way back to Dallas.

Now, we had a connecting flight that we were concerned about, but we should not have been worried, because by the time we got to Dallas, I received a text message telling me that flight had been canceled. So, there was no need to be rushing through the airport. We got tickets the next day on a flight that would take us to Vancouver. It was supposed to leave out at nine o'clock that morning, so we should be fine reaching our destination in time to board the cruise ship.

We went and settled into a hotel for a very short time and then made our way back to the airport at 6 A.M. We were in good shape! Not the leisurely trip we had planned, but still in good shape. Then we received the word that the flight was now delayed until noon. Now it seemed most unlikely that we could catch our ship. The good news is, we made the ship in the final moments. Come to find out we were not the only ones being delayed, so they literally, held the ship for our group of travelers.

Our trip seems to be a little microcosm of the children of Israel in the wilderness. The people of Israel got rerouted, they were in a holding pattern, and they were not able to reach their final destination. It was not because of weather, but it was because of unbelief.

As we are walking with these people in Numbers, we have much to learn. You see, we are very much like these people. They were living between redemption accomplished and redemption consummated. They had been delivered from the bondage of slavery but were not yet in the promised land; they were living in the wilderness.

May I say to you that we are living in a wilderness? Would you agree with me? I would argue that those who do not think we are living in a wilderness have their heads in the sand. Pick up the newspaper, watch the evening reports, or take a glance at social media. There is brokenness, there is hatred, there is division, and there is animosity everywhere you look. We are living in a day when just disagreeing with someone makes you a hater. I want you to know that we are living in a wilderness.

But I also want you to know that in our own spiritual lives, we are right where these people were. You see, we are in between salvation accomplished and salvation consummated. In salvation, there was that beginning phase when we trusted Christ; we have been set free from the penalty of our sin. If we have been saved, one glorious day we are going to be set free from even the presence of sin – that is glorification. But where are we now? We are right now in a wilderness. We are right now in between those two realities, experiencing a process known as sanctification.

As we will learn, it was easier for God to get their hearts out of Egypt than to get Egypt out of their hearts. Would you agree with me? That is my struggle as well; too many times, the world has crept into my heart and into my life. J. Vernon McGee is right when he titles the book of Numbers, "The Pilgrim's Progress." That is a very apt title for this book, where we find the people of God walking, wandering, warring, working, witnessing, and worshiping. They are all doing these things in the wilderness.

Here are a few important things to note as we begin our study of Numbers:

First, the title of the book is "Numbers." That is the English title, and this title comes from the fact that there are two censuses that are taken in the book of Numbers. We find in our text that God instructs Moses to number the men who are twenty years old and upward – everyone who is able to go out to war. God again is preparing his people for the conquest in the promised land. One census is taken at the beginning of the book comprising the first generation of unbelief that will die in the wilderness, and a second census is taken at the end of the book numbering the generation that will enter into the promised land.

"Numbers," though, is not the traditional Hebrew title. The traditional Hebrew title of this book comes from the opening verse, and it is literally "in the wilderness." I think that is a great title for a wilderness book.

Second, who is the author of this book? Traditionally, Moses has been considered by both Jews and Christians as the author of Numbers. Now, when you begin to study deeper, you will find a lot of criticism, critique, and hypotheses about all kinds of putting together of documents and so forth. Still, I believe Moses is the primary author of the book of Numbers, so why do I believe that? The book itself talks about Moses writing this story.

Numbers 33:1-2, "These are the stages of the people of Israel, when they went out of the land of Egypt by their companies under the leadership of Moses and Aaron. Moses wrote down their starting places, stage by stage, by command of the LORD, and these are their stages according to their starting places."

The Scripture says that Moses was writing this down – where they were and what was taking place. Why was he doing this? He was doing this by the command of the Lord.

Numbers 36:13, "These are the commandments and the rules that the LORD commanded through Moses to the people of Israel in the plains of Moab by the Jordan at Jericho."

The Scripture says that Moses, under the inspiration of the Holy Spirit and at the command of the Lord, was writing these things down. For the sake of our meditations here, we are going to say the first five books of the Bible are written by Moses primarily.

Third, how will we outline the book of Numbers? What we find in the book of Numbers is some narrative passages, then laws of purity and laws of holiness, and then more narrative. Why is it written that way?

I think it is written that way to remind the people of Israel that a holy God was dwelling among them. It is going to be seen in even the way that they make their camp. The tabernacle is going to be in the center and every one of the tribes are going to circle that and find their place. They were to be mindful of the fact that a holy God dwelled among them.

How does that relate to us? A holy God is not camped out among us, but the Holy Spirit of God dwells within us. We need to remember that the God who dwells within is just as holy as the Old Testament God that camped among His people.

To outline Numbers, there are a couple of ways to divide the book. First, we could divide it geographically. We could divide it based upon where Israel is and where they have traveled or camped. If so, we could call chapters one through nine: "Israel at Mount Sinai," chapters seven through fourteen: "Israel travels from Sinai to Kadesh Barnea," and chapters fifteen to thirty-six: "Israel wandering in the wilderness due to unbelief." However, I want to divide the book a little bit differently.

Raymond Brown, in his commentary of Numbers in The Bible Speaks Today series, divides the book into five sections. The first section he titles "Getting Ready." This covers chapters one through ten, while they are still at Mount Sinai. God is preparing them.

The second section, from Chapter 10:11 through 12:16, he entitles "Setting Out." The third section, from Chapter 13:1 through 14:45, he entitles, "Drawing Back." He entitles the fourth section "Marking Time" from Chapter 15:1 through 25:18; this is the period of time when the generation of unbelief is going to wander around in the wilderness until they all die away.

Have you thought about what it would look like if we had a map and could just see their footprints? They wandered in that tiny little area for forty years. How they wandered around and around and around and around, and they wandered!

Then I realized: would it not be something if God could show my spiritual journey and footprints? My spiritual journey and footprints would not be one straight, narrow road. It would not be one great upward climb. I guarantee you, like the children of Israel, I have had a lot of detours, a lot of sidetracks, and a lot of time wandering around in unbelief. I am just like the people of Israel.

The final section, according to Raymond Brown, is entitled "Pressing On." The generation of faith rises up and enters into the promised land.

Finally, let us consider the theme of the book of Numbers. I believe the theme of the book is God's faithfulness and man's unfaithfulness. Regardless of the rebellion, the complaining, the grumbling, and all the rest, God did not abandon his people. He demonstrated that He is a covenant-keeping God!

Aren't you glad that God does not treat us the way that we treat him? God is a covenant-keeping God; He keeps every promise He makes. You see, this is not just an ancient book about an ancient people, but it is a glorious picture of our faithful God.

Regardless of what is going on in your life right now, God is faithful, and He keeps all the promises He has made. The promises in the past give confidence for the future.

Trust Him – He is trustworthy!

GETTING READY FOR THE JOURNEY

We have all probably heard the quotation attributed to Ralph Waldo Emerson: "Life is a journey, not a destination." For the children of Israel, I would say it was about both the journey and the destination. The opening of the book of Numbers serves to set our journey in a historical context. This is not a fairy tale. This is not in a land far, far away. These are historical people, and this sets us in our context.

The Exodus story and the wilderness wanderings are foundational to much of the New Testament writers. Sometimes we forget that the Old Testament forms and informs our understanding of God's redeeming love expressed in Christ and His atoning work on the cross. It reminds us that the Scriptures we hold in our hands are not sixty-six independent books, but rather one book unified upon the theme of God's redeeming work among His people.

All the stories of the Bible have one common hero, one coming Messiah, one glorious Lord! Jesus becomes the lens through which we view all Scripture. This is what Jesus taught the two men on the road to Emmaus on that resurrection day.

Luke 24:27: "And beginning with Moses and all the Prophets, he interpreted to them in all the Scriptures the things concerning himself."

We are thinking about getting ready for the journey. The first ten chapters of the book of Numbers all happen at the same place – the setting of it all – Mount Sinai. This is the place where God has brought them. They have been there now for about a year, and God has done marvelous things among them. They have seen the manifestation of the power and the glory of God. They have seen the mountain on fire. They have seen the lightning and heard the thunder. They have heard the voice of God. They have received from the Lord the plans for the tabernacle and the testimony of the law in the Ten Commandments. All this was given to them at Mount Sinai.

They are poised to move forward from this place to the land that God had promised to them. Now, let me ask you this: how do you prepare for a journey? Do you have a certain routine, or are there certain things that you do as you get ready to go on a journey, go on a long vacation, or take a long trip? I know – at our house – there is a certain process that takes place...and I am totally out of it!

Recently, we have packed and unpacked several different times. Packing is one of those things that I am left out of now. The reason is that I oversaw packing once and did not do such a good job. So as a husband, if you fail one time at packing, you do not have to worry about packing any more.

Janey and I have been married long enough that I know one thing for sure: she loves to shop! I have found Janey to also be a little bit on the tricky side. One of our last trips was to the Billy Graham Cove, so – as usual – she was in charge of packing, and she has a process of laying things out and getting everything ready. She loaded up the van as she always does, and we were off on our way to the Billy Graham Cove. We got close to the mountains near Newport, Tennessee, and my wife said, "Oh no!" It is never good to hear your wife say that, so I asked what the matter was. She said, "all of our clothes are hanging in the garage."

Clearly, this was going to be an interesting trip to the Billy Graham Cove! We had one suitcase full of stuff, but our main clothes had been put in a garment bag and left hanging in the garage. Here is the tricky wife part. I said, "well, I guess we are going to have to turn around and go back" to which she replied, "no, maybe not. Is there a mall between here and the Billy Graham Cove?" I said, "well, we pass through Asheville. I imagine that there is a mall somewhere in town." Sure enough, you can guess what happened. Janey got to shop.

Most people have a process for getting ready to go on a trip. Usually, I do not sleep well the night before. I guess it is the anticipation. I do not want to oversleep. I do not want to miss the alarm. I do not want to miss my flight, so the sleeping sometimes is not good the night before a trip.

But as I think about God preparing these people for their journey, there are three simple truths I want to leave with you:

The first truth is "God always prepares His people for the journey."

This is what God is doing in these opening chapters of the book of Numbers. He is preparing His people. He is getting them ready to enter into the promised land. He has been getting them ready, by the way, for a long, long time. (Side note: Aren't you glad that nothing ever occurs to God? He is never taken by surprise.)

God began preparing for this journey all the way back when He called Abram out of Ur of the Chaldeans. He called Abram to come and find a land, and Abram left not knowing where he was going. God made promises to this man Abraham – He made a covenant with him. In Genesis 15, as He made that covenant with Abraham, He told Abraham that his descendants would be strangers in a foreign land and they would serve there for four hundred years, but then He would bring them out.

You see, the whole Exodus story is a part of God's plan. God was preparing His people. One of the great events in Abraham's life was when Abraham was called by God to go up to Mount Moriah and there offer his son Isaac upon that mountain. It is an interesting story. You find it in Genesis 22, but I want to draw your attention to the opening phrase in Genesis 22:1. It says, "It came to pass after these things." When you think about this great test of faith (God had called Abraham up on the mountain to offer his son – the son of promise), I want you to know that this was not the first test Abram had experienced. This was not the first thing that God had called him to do. The massively big test came about after a lot of little tests that God had brought him through preparing him for this big test.

Remember, God always prepares His people for the journey. The reality is that before God ever sent Israel into Egypt, He prepared the way before them. How did he do that? He prepared the way by sending Joseph ahead of them. Those of you who know the story know that Joseph did not choose to go, yet God was at work. Joseph was hated by his brothers and sold by them into slavery. Yet God was orchestrating all of those events, redeeming even the evil worked against Joseph. How wonderful to hear the words of Joseph later, "You meant it for evil, but God meant it for good." You see, our God is a sovereign God who is orchestrating all these events.

God is getting a people ready. He is preparing a people. Before He brought them out of Egypt, He prepared a deliverer by the name of Moses. Before Moses could ever come and lead them out, God had to prepare him. God spent a long time preparing Moses; He spent forty years preparing Moses in Egypt and forty years preparing Moses in the backside of the wilderness. All preparation so that he could be the one to lead the people out of the bondage of Egypt.

Is it not interesting that Moses got a great education while he was in Egypt, and then he got on-the-job training while he was out in the wilderness – the very same wilderness which he will now be leading these people? He was out there for forty years taking care of his father-in-law's sheep. Those were not wasted days; those were days of preparation.

Preparation is vitally important to any success:
"By failing to prepare, you are preparing to fail." – Benjamin Franklin
"Give me six hours to chop down a tree and I will spend the first four to sharpen my axe." – Abraham Lincoln
"When opportunity comes, it's too late to prepare." – John Wooden

I say all this as a reminder to know that our God is the very same God who prepared Abram, Joseph, and Moses. He is a God who prepares us for our journey in life. I want you to know the very same God that had been preparing these people is the very same God who is at work in your life and in my life, and He prepares us for what He calls us to do.

In Numbers 1, we find a story where seventy individuals went into Egypt, and about two million came out. You will notice that the Bible says in verse 46 that the number of males that were twenty years old and upward were 603,550. I imagine if there were that many men that were twenty and up, there would approximately be the same number of women. Then add two or three children per family, and you easily have a number that is estimated over two million people.

Seventy go into Egypt and two million come out! A family goes into Egypt and a nation comes out. God has birthed a nation in Egypt, and He is now ready to bring them into the promised land. He has been preparing them all the way, but some of that preparation was painful. Some of the preparing that the Lord did in their lives was a part of the affliction of their time in Egypt.

This should teach us that God is at work preparing you and me, and many times He prepares us through the means of suffering and adversity. God uses trials and adversity to prepare us and shape us into the image of Christ. Many times, God uses pain to prepare us for what He has called us for and what He has called us to be! Regardless of what you might see or hear from some TV evangelists, all suffering is not because of sin or a lack of faith on your part. Even if you have great faith, you will still suffer. God is using adversity, trial, and suffering to prepare us for future glory and service.

The Apostle Peter wrote in 1 Peter 1:6-7, "In this you rejoice, though now for a little while, if necessary, you have been grieved by various trials, so that the tested genuineness of your faith—more precious than gold that perishes though it is tested by fire—may be found to result in praise and glory and honor at the revelation of Jesus Christ".

What is it that Peter is saying? Peter is saying life is hard and there are going to be difficult things. But I want you to know that as a child of God, you can understand that even the adversity and the suffering that comes in your life has meaning and purpose. God is using it to prepare you for where He is going to take you in this journey. Remember that we are on a wilderness journey much like the Israelites.

This life can be difficult, but for the child of God, He has a purpose in the pain, and He alone can redeem our suffering for His glory. God is using it to mold us and to form us and to fashion us into the likeness of the Lord Jesus Christ. He is using it to prepare us. That is the reason why Peter could say we greatly rejoice, even though in a season of weary and heaviness, this seems like a contradiction. But as a child of God, we can rejoice even in our momentary temptations and trials because we know that they are working for us.

I think this is what Paul meant in 2 Corinthians 4:17 by "our light affliction." Now when you go on and read in 2 Corinthians 11, you find out that his "light afflictions" were being stoned, beaten with rods, shipwrecked, and so on. He refers to them as our light afflictions, which are for but a moment working for us a far more exciting and eternal weight of glory. Life is difficult. Life is hard. Adversity does come. Trials, sickness, and suffering are a part of our present experience, but we know that our God is sovereign over them. I heard Charles Stanley say many, many years ago that, "everything that comes into our life as a child of God is – first of all – filtered through the hands of a loving God." God has a purpose, and therefore we can rejoice.

How do I know that suffering comes even to those who are in the will of God? The Bible is full of those examples. Consider a man by the name of Job. We know Job and think about all his suffering, but in the opening chapters, we are privy to developments that were going on in the heavenlies. The fact of the matter is, Job was not suffering because of his sin. He was suffering because he was a shining example of a man who loved God and hated evil, a man who the Bible says was even offering sacrifices for his grown children in case they may have sinned. He was a man of integrity, a man of righteousness, a man that was godly and right before the Lord, but he suffered.

Some say if you have enough faith you will not suffer; however, consider the Apostle Paul. I believe if anybody had faith, it was Paul, but he had a thorn in the flesh and prayed concerning this ailment and affliction. Guess what? God did not choose to remove it. Instead, God said to Paul, "My grace is sufficient for you." Surely, God's grace is sufficient for us as well.

There is a second truth that I want you to see: "Conquest seldom – if ever – comes without conflict."

Where do you see this in the text? Why are they taking this census repeatedly? God says, "I want you to number the men that are twenty years and older that are able to go out to war." You see, God is building an army! He is preparing them for war. He understands that they are going to be entering into the promised land. The Lord is going to fight for them, and God is going to do marvelous things among them, but they will also have conflict.

May I remind you in our wilderness journey that we also are in a conflict? The simple truth is the Christian life is not lived on a playground, but it is lived on a battlefield. That is the reason why the apostle Paul would say to the church at Ephesus that they needed to put on the whole armor of God, because we have an enemy. We have an adversary, and you are foolish if you think for one minute that he is not out to destroy your marriage, your home, your testimony, and your witness. He is hard at work!

We need to recognize this reality. We need to put on the whole armor of God. We need to understand that there is indeed a conflict. We have an enemy. I think that is the reason why Paul would say to Timothy, "Share in suffering as a good soldier of Christ Jesus" (2 Timothy 2:3)

Please know, whenever you think about this Christian life being a warfare, that the greatest enemy we face is not other people. It is not anyone that is out in the world. The greatest enemy I face is "inside of me." It is that indwelling sin. It is the old man that is still there. You see, we face three great enemies: the devil, the world, and the flesh. But the one that I struggle with the most is the flesh – it is the man I see in the mirror each morning!

I would encourage you to do some reading from a man by the name of John Owen. He was one of the old Puritan writers. John Owen is famous for a quote concerning indwelling sin: "Be killing sin or sin will be killing you." Now that is a wonderful quote! I have seen it on shirts, plaques, and even tattoos. I have seen it featured in many ways, but it was not just a catchy platitude with John Owen.

John Owen wrote a great work called The Mortification of Sin. In this book he wrote, "Let no man pretend to fear sin that does not fear temptation. Also, these two are closely united, too closely united to be separated." He also wrote, "He does not truly hate the root who delights in the fruit. Let no man think that he can kill sin with a few easy, gentle strokes. He who has once smitten a serpent, if he will not follow up this blow until he be slain, may repent that he ever began the quarrel."

In other words, there is a struggle that is to go on, and we must be engaged in that struggle. We must be making war on the sin that is within us. Let me ask you what areas of your life are you presently making war against? Your thought life? Your relationships? Your attitudes? Your choices, your desires, or your affections? We need to be making war on sin, for conquest never comes without conflict.

There is a third truth I want you to understand: "The presence of God is a glorious reality when you are in the wilderness!"

The children of Israel were going to be moving throughout the wilderness. Every time that they broke camp and every time that they came back together, the tribes were to be arranged in the same order and location. God, by the way, is a God of order. He ordered the arrangement of the troops and the tribes around the encampment.

Can you imagine the chaos it would have been if every time that they broke camp and traveled somewhere, everyone would have been jockeying for a better position? Everyone would have wanted to be at the head. Everyone would have been trying to find a better place, but God ordered it. In his ordering of it, did you notice what was at the very center? The tabernacle – or tent of meeting.

The tabernacle was a reminder to the people of Israel throughout all of their wilderness journeys that God was dwelling among them. That is a glorious reality! All the hardships, all the suffering, and all the difficulties would be bearable because God was dwelling among them. They were never to forget that a holy God was in their midst. This is a frightful thought!

Look at what Numbers 1:53 says, "But the Levites shall camp around the tabernacle of the testimony, so that there may be no wrath on the congregation of the people of Israel. And the Levites shall keep guard over the tabernacle of the testimony."

Indeed, every time they established camp, right in the center was the tabernacle, a reminder that a holy God was among them. But this God was not a casual God. The invitation was not for anyone to come any time that they pleased. They could only come God's way!

In my spiritual journey, the most comforting reality is also the most convicting reality. You know what that is? It is the presence of the Holy Spirit with me 24/7. There is nothing more comforting than that. In the wee hours of the night when your heart is broken or when you have gotten a call that has left you so distraught, just to know that the Lord is with you - what a comfort!

In all honesty, though, I want to also tell you there are times I would like to be able to take the Holy Spirit and put Him in a closet for a little while, because there are some things that Tony wants to do, some attitudes that I want to hold on to, or some sinful desire I want to pursue. The most convicting thing is that the presence of God does not dwell in a sanctuary, but in the life of the believer.

Oh, if we ever fully get ahold of this, it will change our Mondays, Tuesdays and Wednesdays. It will change what we click on with the mouse. It will change how we respond. It will change our appetites. It will change everything. Why? Because the Spirit of the living God does not dwell in the midst of the camp or the community, He dwells inside every believer. What a challenging thing! What a comforting thing! What a glorious thing when you are walking through the wilderness!

These Israelites did not know what was ahead of them, but they did know that God was with them. I do not know what your journey will hold. I do not know what the future is going to bring in your life and, in your situation, but I do know this: God is among us. God dwells within us, and He has given us a promise that He will never leave us nor forsake us. That is good news – glorious news – that he is with us 24/7 (even those times when we wish he were not). He is with us.

May we be challenged by this reality. In the workplace, the Lord is with you. When you are choosing what to watch on the television, the Lord is with you. When you are clicking your computer mouse, the Lord is with you. What a comforting, challenging thought! I want you to know that we can make it in this wilderness because we have the Lord with us.

Listen to what Paul wrote to the church at Rome:

Romans 8:31-39, "What shall we say to these things? If God is for us, who can be against us? He who did not spare his own Son but gave him up for us all? How will he not also with him graciously give us all things? Who shall bring any charge against God's elect? It is God who justifise. Who is to condemn? Christ. Jesus is the one who died—more than that, who was raised-- who is at the right hand of God, who indeed is interceding for us. Who shall separate us from the love of Christ? Shall tribulation, or distress, or persecution, or famine, or nakedness, or danger, or sword (or your situation or my situation, will it separate us from the love of Christ)? As it is written, 'For your sake we are being killed all the day long; we are regarded as sheep to be slaughtered.' No, in all these things we are more than conquerors through him who loved us For I am sure that neither death nor life, nor angels nor rulers, nor things present, nor things to come, nor powers, nor height nor depth, nor anything else in all creation, will be able to separate us from the love of God in Christ Jesus, our Lord."

He is with us – the presence of God is with us in our wilderness experience – and nothing will ever separate us from the love of God.

WARNING: SERVING GOD IS SERIOUS

What is God like? This is a question that almost every human being (at least those that believe there is a God) has contemplated at one time or another. The ways in which we think about God are very important. You see, there are many that simply imagine a god of their own design. In doing so, they are guilty of idolatry – worshipping a false god which is a figment of their imaginations. This is clear in the commonly heard statement, "My god would never …" That is the problem – they have created a god that is palatable for them.

Numbers chapters 3-4 reveal several realities concerning the God of the Bible. As we learned in chapter 2, many people see it as a very mundane chapter with a lot of names and tribes, but as the Scripture reminds us – all Scripture is given by inspiration of God. There is much to be gleaned from such a chapter.

God's arrangement of the tribes of Israel with the tabernacle in the center was no accident. These were the redeemed people of God, and He was in their midst. God communicated with them. He spoke to them. God gave them instruction. God has a purpose in all that He does! Even the ordering of the tribes around the camp was by divine design. God had a reason and a purpose for putting them in their places.

Chapters 3-4 deal with the priesthood – the Levitical priesthood. God is now appointing and setting aside one tribe – the tribe of Levi – and they are given the assignment of taking care of all things related to the tabernacle. God chose them and appointed them with the task of overseeing everything related to worship, which was central to the people of God.

As we are looking at these chapters, we are once again reminded that our God is a God that has meticulous order and gives care concerning everything that He does. He is not a haphazard God. He is a God that has a reason and a design for all that He does. Scriptures clearly reveal that we must approach God in the way God has instructed and prescribed. In other words, we are not free to come to God on our own terms and in our own way.

That is in great contrast to the evangelical church in America! Scriptures would indicate that serving and worshipping God is very serious. Do you think that in America today we take worship and the service of God as seriously as we should?

I am convinced that one of our problems in America – and in the church in America today – is that we have lost sight of the holiness of God. Therefore, because we have lost sight of the holiness of God, the approaching of God, the service of God, and the worshiping of God have become extremely trite and casual. In fact, I recently read of two churches: one that was building a "helter-skelter" amusement ride in the middle of their church, and another that was putting in a putt-putt course to attract people to worship.

Brothers and sisters, I would submit to you that we are not in that kind of business. God is a God who is holy, and He must be approached in the means that God has ordained and instructed us. I understand there is joy, and I understand there should be excitement. There should be love and peace and all these things, but it should always be an awesome reality to think about the fact that we are approaching and worshipping the holy God of the universe. We should always approach God with the respect and the reverence that He deserves. Let us consider our text in Numbers as there are four points I wish to share.

First, I want you to notice this: "God appoints leadership."

In Numbers 1:47-51, we find these words, "But the Levites were not listed along with them by their ancestral tribe. For the LORD spoke to Moses, saying, 'Only the tribe of Levi you shall not list, and you shall not take a census of them among the people of Israel. But appoint the Levites over the tabernacle of the testimony, and over all its furnishings, and over all that belongs to it. They are to carry the tabernacle and all its furnishings, and they shall take care of it and shall camp around the tabernacle. When the tabernacle is to set out, the Levites shall take it down, and when the tabernacle is to be pitched, the Levites shall set it up. And if any outsider comes near, he shall be put to death.'"

The Levites were appointed by God to be the guardians of the tabernacle. They were responsible for tearing it down and setting it up. These days a lot of churches begin as church plants, and in their early days, they often meet in a school gymnasium or other shared community space. Part of that arrangement requires that somebody show up early in the morning and set out all the equipment. They must set up the sound system and the chairs and all the other things. It all must be put together before people arrive for worship and then after worship is over – some time that day – they must pack it all up and store it somewhere.

That gives you some notion as to what was going on here for the Levites. Again, these were people on the move. Every time that they moved, the tabernacle had to be torn down, had to be carried, and then had to be reconstructed. This was not a task that was given to just anyone. They did not vote on this. They did not choose who was going to do this. God appointed the Levites and gave them this responsibility. God sovereignly selects whomever He wishes to serve Him in His kingdom's work today.

Often today, we hear of people deciding to pursue Christian ministry as though it is like any other vocation choice. Perhaps this is why many who start out never persevere to the end. For me, it was no choice or pursuit. I felt the call of God upon my life. God called me to "preach" – and in that day, this was expressed by announcing that God had called you to preach.

I want you to know that this was not something that I sought after. In fact, this was something that I resisted. This is not what I wanted to do for my vocation. If you had asked me then, I was going to be an architect. I had taken drafting courses in high school, and I was planned to be an architect...but God called me to preach His gospel.

I knew God was calling me to preach, but I tried to appease God by doing everything in the church except preach. In my little church, I taught Sunday school when I was just a teenager. I was the Sunday school superintendent. I sang in the choir. I would have even led the choir if they had let me - anything other than preaching.

This place of service at the tabernacle was one the Levites did not solicit. They were not elected by the rest of the tribes to get this responsibility. God selected them. Now the question might arise, why would God select the Levites and give them this responsibility? Certainly, we recognize that God did not choose the tribe of Levi because Levi was a perfect, upright individual. Levi – along with his brother Simeon – was guilty of some terrible crimes. They were guilty of some violent acts of cruelty which you can read in Genesis 34. They were also a party to selling their brother Joseph into slavery. In other words, these were not sinless men.

I would remind you that if the only men God could call into the ministry were sinless men, he would have none to call. We all have flaws, and we all have sinned. But know that God, in His sovereign will, chose Levi.

The second point I want to share is: "God demands holiness."

As we look at Numbers 3:1-4, we are reminded of an event that demonstrates the holiness of God and the seriousness of worshiping Him. Moses records it as follows:

"These are the generations of Aaron and Moses at the time when the LORD spoke with Moses on Mount Sinai. These are the names of the sons of Aaron: Nadab the firstborn, and Abihu, Eleazar, and Ithamar. These are the names of the sons of Aaron, the anointed priests, whom he ordained to serve as priests. But Nadab and Abihu died before the LORD when they offered unauthorized fire before the LORD in the wilderness of Sinai, and they had no children. So Eleazar and Ithamar served as priests in the lifetime of Aaron their father."

These verses simply state that Nadab and Abihu died before the Lord. Why did this happen? What were they guilty of doing? They offered what the Bible describes as "strange fire" before the Lord. Now, if we look back to Leviticus 10:1-3, we find the account of this event. To understand the context of this divine judgment upon the sons of Aaron, we need to look back one verse to Leviticus 9:24 to see what is going on:

"And fire came out from before the LORD and consumed the burnt offering and the pieces of fat on the altar, and when all the people saw it, they shouted and fell on their faces."

Remember, these chapters and verses tell a cohesive story, so we continue with Nadab and Abihu, the sons of Aaron, in Leviticus 10. They took their respective fire pans, put fire in them, placed incense on it, and offered strange fire before the Lord "which He had not commanded them." Those final six words are vitally important to notice. The fire came out from the presence of the Lord and consumed Nadab and Abihu, and they died before the Lord.

This is one of the times in Scripture where God chooses to make an example of someone to drive home the point that He is holy and cannot be approached in any means other than what He has instructed. The next verse says:

"Then Moses said to Aaron, 'This is what the Lord has said. 'Among those who are near me I will be sanctified, and before the people I will be glorified.' And Aaron held his peace."

Aaron was not even allowed to mourn or grieve over the loss of his sons! This may seem harsh and cruel, but God is reminding them – and us as well – to approach Him in the means that He has prescribed, and that He is indeed a holy God.

There is another account in Scripture that drives this home. In 2 Samuel 6, you find King David having a great desire (I think it was a well-intentioned desire) to bring the Ark of the Covenant home to Jerusalem. So, David sent for the Ark of the Covenant...but he should have read the instructions. David was a man after all, and we know men do not like to read instructions. We do not need instructions!

You see, the Lord had told them how the ark was to be transported. There were rods and holders by which the ark was to be carried, and only certain families could carry the ark of the covenant. David did not read those instructions, and he sent men to get the ark and put it on a cart, which they were pulling with an ox. The Bible says that the ox stumbled, and the ark of the covenant began to slide off the cart. Here we learn about a man by the name of Uzza. We probably would never have heard of this man – except for the fact that he reached out and took hold of the ark of the covenant.

You and I would probably have done the same thing if we had been there. He saw the ark of the covenant sliding off from the cart, and he reached out and touched it to steady it. The Bible says God struck him dead, and we might say that was very extreme. I want you to know that our holy God is not to be taken lightly. Again, we are to approach Him in a means which He has instructed.

What exactly did Nadab and Abihu do? We are not sure. It just says they offered strange fire. Some scholars believe they offered it at the wrong time. It says the Lord had not commanded it, and maybe they were presumptuous in doing this. Perhaps they received the fire from the wrong place. God designed the tabernacle in such a way that the fire from the altar was to be taken into the altar of incense. It had to come from the right place, so perhaps they got a fire from the wrong source. Perhaps they offered it with the wrong attitude.

I do not know what exactly they did, but I do know that God judged them severely. These accounts in the Scripture remind us – I believe and repeat – that a holy God must be approached in a way He instructs us. We are not to freelance. We are not to think that we can come to God on our terms. We must come by the way of the cross. There is no way to shortcut or substitute for what God has ordained. The only way we can ever approach a holy God is through the Lord Jesus Christ! For all of us are unholy – it is only in the righteousness of Christ that we can approach a holy God.

F.B. Meyer, once wrote, "We must take care. Lest we ever introduce strange fire into our Worship, the fire of your own emotions, enthusiasm, or excitement, we must not rush carelessly into the divine presence." In other words, I am convinced that we cannot just come to God on our own terms and think God is going to be pleased with whatever we offer Him as far as service and worship. It must be offered to Him in reverence and with an understanding of His holiness. We must prepare our hearts before we come before a holy God.

I am also convinced that many times we do more preparation on the outside to come to church than we do on the inside. How much time do you spend looking in the mirror, showering, shaving, getting prepared, and getting your clothes on? Let me ask you, how does that compare to the amount of time you spent looking inwardly and asking the Lord to prepare your heart for worship? We need to approach Him in the way and the manner and the attitude that reflects His holiness and our worship of Him.

The third thing that I want to share is "God's servants must be redeemed."

In Numbers 3:40-51, we read some strange things that are hard for us to understand. In these verses, the Lord is substituting the tribe of Levi for the firstborn of the nation of Israel. It is a strange text to us with this whole concept of being ransomed or redeemed, so it is hard for us to figure it all out, but God is doing a marvelous thing here. God is pointing back to the Passover. Recall that through the Passover – because God spared them – every firstborn of every household belonged to the Lord. Now, the Lord, rather than taking the firstborn of every household, chooses one tribe to be a substitute for the firstborn of all the nation of Israel. That is why there is the numbering.

Remember, we said the book of Numbers got its name because of the census or the numbering of the people. Now, in the first census, they did not number the tribe of Levi. Why? Because this is a number of men, twenty and above, able to go to war. But that doesn't mean the tribe of Levi did not get numbered. In chapters three and four, they got numbered twice. They were counted, first of all, everyone a month old and upward, and then another counting, or census, of those that were 30 to 50. Now, why these censuses? Why the numbering of Levi?

The numbering of those a month old and upward is because of this redemption that was taking place. It says in Numbers 3:45, "Take the Levites instead of all the first born among the people of Israel, and the cattle of the Levites instead of their cattle. The Levites shall be mine: I am the Lord."

And then he goes on to say, "And as the redemption price for the 273 of the firstborn of the people of Israel, over and above the number of male Levites, you shall take five shekels per head; you shall take them according to the shekel of the sanctuary and give the money to Aaron and his sons as the redemption price for those who are over."

So, here's what happened: they counted all the firstborn of the other tribes and got a number. They counted all of those one month and older of the Levites. They got a number. There were two hundred and seventy-three more of the firstborn of the eleven tribes than there were of Levites. So, the two hundred and seventy-three firstborn now are going to be ransomed by the paying of a ransom fee. They were to pay five shekels per person.

This is to ransom them. And this money was given to Aaron for the carrying out of the priesthood and the work. You see, God was again doing something marvelous. We probably could never tie it all together, but He was teaching them two things: redemption and substitution.

When we think about what God has done in our lives, we need to praise God for redemption and substitution. In the New Testament, we were not redeemed with silver and gold as God was redeeming people here with five shekels per head. We have not been redeemed with silver and gold, but we have been redeemed by the precious blood of the Lord Jesus Christ.

But where does that substitution come in? For the nation of Israel, every time they saw the Levites carrying out the work, it was a visual aid reminding them that they were serving in place of the first born of every household – a visual reminder of being a substitute for them. Praise the Lord that Jesus Christ is our substitute! A man that knew no sin was made sin on our behalf, the Lord laid on Him the iniquity of us all, and He died in our place. He tasted death for every man.

Praise the Lord that – when we think about our relationship with God – redemption and substitution are primary and key to our understanding what God has done in our life. God is foreshadowing all of that in what He is doing here among his people in Numbers.

The final thing to share: "God's work is vast, diverse and often tedious."

Numbers 4 records for us all the assignments concerning the movement of the tabernacle. The massive work involved was divided among three families, and each one of these families was given explicit responsibilities. Aaron and his sons covered everything – the ark of the covenant, the table of shortbread, and the altar of incense – in the designated cloth. It was the family of Kohath who had the responsibility of transporting them. If anyone else had touched any of those items, the Lord's judgment would have been upon them, but they alone had the responsibility of carrying them. The Gershonites had the responsibility of carrying all the tabernacle coverings - the tent itself, all the curtains, all the screens, and all the fabric. Another family then had the responsibility of carrying the framework, the pillars, and the sockets.

Every time that the cloud or the pillar of fire moved, they broke camp and moved with it. Everyone knew what they were to do. Everyone had a place. Everyone had a part. God was distributing that labor, and God was giving everyone some responsibility and something to do. He was very meticulous in laying all of this out.

Unlike in the Old Testament, where it was only the tribe of Levi that could serve in the ministry, today, the redeemed people of God have the Spirit of the Lord dwelling inside of us, have been gifted, and have a work to do in the kingdom. As we close this chapter, what do we take away from here?

For one thing, we should remember worship and service to the Lord should be taken more seriously than we do today. Would you agree with me? I think it is heartbreaking in the American church today to see how low a view we have of God and worship. We need to recognize that if we are going to worship God, we should take it seriously because God takes it seriously. We should understand that He is holy. We should approach Him with reverence and fear and awe.

The second thing is we can only approach God in the manner that He has directed us. I know today we live in a world where seemingly "all roads lead to heaven," but the reality is we must come to God in the means and the manner that He has prescribed. There is no way other than the cross. Jesus is the way, the truth, and the life. No one comes to the father but by Him. We cannot approach God in any way other than He has directed us.

Lastly, the work of God involves everyone doing their part. Everyone has a place. Everyone has a responsibility in the work of the kingdom today.

Where are you serving?

How are you using your gifts that God has gifted you with?

Where are you engaged and plugged in?

How are you doing your part for the kingdom?

LET THERE BE LIGHT

Numbers chapter 7 ends with this verse, "And when Moses went into the tent of meeting to speak with the LORD, he heard the voice speaking to him from above the mercy seat that was on the ark of the testimony, from between the two cherubim; and it spoke to him."

In chapter 7, there was a festival, twelve days of giving, during which each one of the tribes came and presented an offering before the Lord. This was an offering that was to be used in the service of the tabernacle. Each of the tribes had an appointed day with each one bringing gifts, and then the Lord distributed the gifts among the Levites according to the service that they rendered.

In the last verse of chapter 7, though, we find God communing with Moses. God spoke to him again at the end of the days of the presentation of these offerings. The Bible says that Moses entered the tent of meeting and the Lord spoke to him. What an incredible thing that God would choose to speak to mere mortal man! How wonderful that God chose to speak to us, and He has spoken to us fully in the revelation of holy Scripture. He speaks to us also through the indwelling of the Holy Spirit.

If God had not spoken, we would know nothing about God. As we now consider the subject of "light," we would be totally "in the dark" concerning God and the things of God had it not been for the fact that God chose to reveal Himself to us. God is a God that has revealed Himself. He is a God who has spoken.

In Numbers, God spoke to Moses in an audible voice. It is said that He was speaking from above the mercy seat – between the two cherubim there in the Holy of Holies. God spoke with Moses as He has never spoken to man before or after. The communication between the Lord and Moses was unique. The Bible says in Deuteronomy 34:10, "And there arose not a prophet since in Israel like unto Moses, whom the Lord knew face to face." The relationship that the Lord and Moses had was incredible. The Lord spoke to Moses and gave him instruction.

In the opening verses of chapter 8, we hear what the Lord spoke. He spoke to Moses concerning light. He spoke to Moses concerning the lamp stand that was to be in the holy place. Remember, the tabernacle was basically a tent -- a rectangular tent that was divided by a veil on the inside. The Ark of the Covenant, which was a chest that was overlaid in gold, was in the Holy of Holies. On the top of the ark was the mercy seat, and on the ends of the mercy seat were two angels whose wings were almost touching. This was the holy dwelling place, and the high priest could only enter once a year into the Holy of Holies.

On the other side of that veil – also enclosed in the tent – was the Holy Place. Inside the Holy Place, there were three pieces of furniture right in front of the veil: the altar of incense, the table of show bread (or the bread of presence), and the lamp stand. The Lord in Numbers 8 is spoke to Moses concerning the lamp stand, and He gave him instructions concerning it.

The first thing that I want you to notice is: "God gave instructions concerning the need for physical light."

Imagine being inside this tabernacle tent. There were no windows and no openings for the light to come in, as the tabernacle itself was made up of four layers of thick material. The inner layer was made up of fine linen and covered with the woven cloth of goat hair. Two layers covered over the top made of ram skins, and then a waterproof covering, made from the skins of porpoises, totaling four thick layers.

Can you imagine being inside with no windows and no way for the light to penetrate through these four layers of coverings? You can imagine how dark that would be, but our God is not a God of darkness. He is a God of light. The Lord provides for His people, and He provided for the priests who were in the Holy Place carrying out their functions and activities. God instructed that there be seven lampstands within the Holy Place, because there was a need for light.

Scientifically speaking, light is a form of electromagnetic radiation – a wavelength which is detectable by the human eye. It exists in a stream of mass-less particles, called photons, each traveling in a wave-like pattern, and it is measured in terms of brightness, color, and temperature. That is a very basic definition of light for you.

Light is essential – it is necessary for life. When God got ready to begin His work of creation, the Bible records that in Genesis 1:3, "God said, 'Let there be light.'" God made a statement. He spoke the universe into existence, and the first thing He created was light. In the next verse, the Bible declares that God saw that the light was good, and God separated the light from the darkness. When God began His creative work, it began with light.

Light is necessary. Many times, architects must choose between form and function. When you think of God and the things that God has made, I want you to know He has both form and function in mind. The function of the lampstand was to provide light inside the Holy Place for the priests to see and carry on their ministry. God is also concerned with the form, though. The form of the lampstand is a thing of beauty; God crafted it in such a way that it reflects His glory. God used both form and function when He placed the lampstand in the tabernacle. Without this presence of light, the tabernacle would be a place of total darkness.

We live in a broken world, sometimes a very dark place. Can you imagine, though, how dark it would be without the Light of Christ – the one True Light – that came into the world? Aren't you glad that God shines upon His people today? Rejoice that His face is turned toward us as the Aaronic blessing reminds us:

Numbers 6:22-27, "The LORD spoke to Moses, saying, 'Speak to Aaron and his sons, saying, 'Thus you shall bless the people of Israel: you shall say to them, The LORD bless you and keep you; the LORD make his face to shine upon you and be gracious to you; the LORD lift up his countenance upon you and give you peace.' So shall they put my name upon the people of Israel, and I will bless them.'"

In this troubled, broken world, nothing is more encouraging than the blessing of the Lord!

The light in the Holy Place reminded the priests of the presence of God. Every time we come into the sanctuary (or the worship center), we need to be mindful of the presence of God. The wonderful thing about God is that He is not limited to a building. As born-again followers of Christ, we are now the temple of the Holy Spirit. We have the presence of God dwelling inside us on Monday morning, on Saturday night, and all throughout the week. Everywhere we go, God dwells among His people.

The most challenging and comforting reality in this life is the indwelling of the Spirit within His people. The greatest accountability partner that you will ever have as a believer is the presence of the Holy Spirit living inside you. You see, a deacon cannot be assigned to you 24/7. The pastor will not be with you around the clock. However, you cannot escape the presence of the Holy Spirit of God that lives inside you. He is with you every moment of every day.

Not only is there necessity for physical light, but there is a great need today for spiritual light. Would you agree with me? I believe with all my heart that we are living in one of the darkest days in America's history. It is mind-blowing to me that we are conceivably the most enlightened generation to have ever lived, but we are in spiritual darkness – perhaps more so than ever before.

It is amazing the knowledge that we have at our fingertips. We can ask "Siri," and she gives us the answer. We can ask "Alexa," and she will tell us all kinds of information. It is amazing what is at our fingertips. Our little children carry around tablets and phones with more information than our forefathers had in all their lifetime! But...do you think that we are wiser than we used to be?

It seems to me that America is getting darker by the moment, and the reason is that we have rejected the light that God has given to us. When you reject the light and the truth, it will only get darker and darker. The Bible has a great deal to say about light and dark and how these two things are illustrations of good and evil. They are contrasted with one another throughout the Scripture.

I was searching for a good definition of darkness. As we established, light is electromagnetic waves that are perceivable by a human eye, but what exactly is darkness? Peter Haig was a scientist, communicator, and writer who said of darkness, "It is a human perception, darkness exists when you cannot perceive any light." He goes on to say, "if you measure light using scientific instruments like a solar cell or a photomultiplier tube, then darkness exists, when you're measured signal is so low that it cannot be distinguished from the ever-present electrical noise." Did you get all that? There will be a quiz at the end of this chapter.

It was the next paragraph that he wrote that caught my attention. "Either way, darkness is not an entity of itself, it is a situation. Darkness is a condition, a condition that exists when there is no light." This is coming from a scientist, and he is saying – when you talk about darkness – it is not a real entity. It is simply a state of affairs. It is a condition.

Darkness is the absence of light, and I believe with all my heart that we need more spiritual light in America. Would you agree? I know we have a lot going for us, but we sure have turned our back on truth and light, and we are living in the darkness.

Let us think about this light for a minute. God is light. God is light by His very character and nature. God is absolute light. The Bible says in 1 John 1:5, "This is the message we have heard from him and proclaim to you, that God is light, and in him is no darkness at all." There is absolutely no darkness in God. There is not a shadow of darkness. It is His nature, and it is revealed in His character. He is absolute holiness, and that is the reason God began the universe by saying, "let there be light," and there was light.

The light of God that was there at the beginning will be there at the end of this earthly story as well. In Revelation 22:5, we read "And night will be no more. They will need no light of lamp or sun, for the Lord God will be their light, and they will reign forever and ever." God is light, and God sent light into the world. The Bible declares in the Gospel of John 1:1: "In the beginning was the Word, and the Word was with God, and the Word was God. He was in the beginning with God. All things were made through him, and without him was not anything made that was made. In him was life; and the life was the light of men. The light shines in the darkness, and the darkness has not overcome it."

Darkness will never prevail over the light. The only time that darkness prevails is when there is a diminishing of the light. As soon as the light is turned on, the darkness flees. It is the removal of the light that creates the darkness. In the John 8:12, Jesus said, "I am the light of the world. Whoever follows me will not walk in darkness, but will have the light of life."

Simeon understood that Jesus is the Light, and upon seeing the young Messiah said, "Now you are letting your servant depart in peace, according to your word; for my eyes have seen your salvation that you have prepared in the presence of all peoples, a light for revelation to the Gentiles, and for glory to your people." (Luke 2:29-32)

John the Baptist knew Jesus as the light. John 1:6-9 says "There was a man sent from God, whose name was John. He came as a witness, to bear witness about the light, that all might believe through him. He was not the light, but came to bear witness about the light. The true light, which gives light to everyone, was coming into the world."

Jesus, the Son of God, is the true Light. This light serves to reveal our sin! From John 3, beginning with the most quoted and familiar verse in the Bible, "For God so loved the world, that he gave his only Son, that whoever believes in him should not perish, but have eternal life." It continues, "For God did not send his Son into the world to condemn the world: but in order that the world might be saved through him. Whoever believes in him is not condemned, but whoever does not believe is condemned already, because he has not believed in the name of the only Son of God."

Do not miss this! If you have not believed upon the Lord Jesus Christ, you are not waiting for some day of judgment to be condemned. You are already abiding under condemnation because you have refused to believe on the name of the only begotten Son of God. "And this is the judgment: the light has come into the world, and people loved the darkness rather than the light because their works were evil. For everyone who does wicked things hates the light and does not come to the light, lest his works should be exposed. But whoever does what is true comes to the light, so that it may be clearly seen that his works have been carried out in God." (John 3:19-21) In other words, listen! The light is necessary to expose our sin.

The reason we need to focus on the holiness of God is that when we come before Him, we recognize that we are not holy. When I look upon the holiness of God, I never feel good about myself. It is like looking into the mirror. You might look good when you check the mirror in a dim room, but when you turn the lights on and look in the mirror closely, the flaws are harder to hide. The light of God and His Word exposes our sin so that we will cry out to Jesus for the cleansing and forgiveness we need.

Repentance is turning away from your sin and embracing the Savior. Seeing the beauty of Christ: the same light that shines and shows me my sin is the light that shows me the gospel in the grace of Christ. We need the light. How desperately we need the light!

Finally, consider this: "God's light is given to be shared."

Those of us who are walking in the light know what we are supposed to be doing – shining the light in this dark world. I am convinced that part of the reason America has gotten so dark is that Christians who have the light are not shining the light. We are not being bold for Christ. We are hiding in our churches, and we are not talking about Christ throughout the week. We are not letting the light shine.

The Bible says in Matthew 5:14-16, "You are the light of the world. A city set on a hill cannot be hidden. Nor do people light a lamp and put it under a basket, but on a stand, and it gives light to all in the house. In the same way, let your light shine before others, so that they may see your good works and give glory to your Father who is in heaven."

What did you do this past week that glorified the Father? What did you do this past week that allowed the light of Christ to shine? What did you do this week that brought honor and glory to your heavenly Father? Whatever your answer, do more of it this coming week!

THE LORD WHO DELIVERS ALSO DIRECTS

Time to move! Do you enjoy moving? The sorting, the rearranging, the packing, the loading, the unloading, and then the looking for what you need. There are few things that I dislike more than moving! Well, perhaps the whole car trading business – I really dislike that process.

The story continues with the children of Israel, and it brings us to a transition point in the Book of Numbers. From Numbers 9 forward, we will find them on the move with the Lord leading them and guiding them. Up unto this point, there has been a constant refrain, "and the people did all according to the word of the Lord." There has been a great deal of obedience on the part of the people of God. They have spent the last year camped out around the Mount of God and were now celebrating their second Passover - the first outside of the land of Egypt. It marked one year since God had delivered them from the bondage of slavery.

It is now time to move. The Lord is about to lead His people to the door of the Promised Land. While there had been a great deal of obedience, from this point forward, there will be a great deal of disobedience on the part of the people of God. There will be much recorded in the coming chapters about rebellion, defiance, and a lack of faith. There will be accounts of them grumbling and complaining along the way.

The good news is that the God who delivered them from Egypt's bondage is the same God who would faithfully be with them throughout all their journey. That is the reason why I have entitled this chapter "The Lord Who Delivers Also Directs." Even though they were a grumbling people, a complaining people, even at times a rebellious and disobedient people, the Lord remains faithful to them. His presence did not abandon them in the journey – the Lord went with them.

The main truth of Numbers 9:15-23 is: "The Lord who brings us out is the Lord who will bring us through."

Are you grateful and thankful that the sovereign hand of God that has delivered you out of the bondage of sin is the same sovereign hand that is guiding you in the journey of this life? The good news is God does not abandon us. Even when we are a rebellious bunch, even when we too are disobedient, even when we lack the faith to step out and move when God tells us to move, even though we are much like the people of Israel, God stays with us. Praise the Lord!

In Numbers 9, we see the picture of the Passover – which is a beautiful illustration of how we have been set free from our sin – followed by a passage describing the cloud by day and the pillar of fire by night with which God was leading his people. Salvation is not the end; it is the beginning! Sometimes we get things so fouled up; we think that once we have made a profession of faith and been baptized, that is the end of it. No, that is only the beginning of it.

Salvation is the beginning of eternal life. That is the beginning of the journey for us as believers. We are all pilgrims and strangers in this present life. We need the direction of the Lord. We need the guidance of the Lord. We need the Lord to be with us in our journey – for we are easily lost without Him. Have you ever gotten lost on your journey? Sure, we all have. We – like the people of Israel – desperately need the Lord.

The Lord provided His people with His continual presence. It says in verse 15, "Now, on the day that the tabernacle was erected, the cloud covered the tabernacle, the tent of meeting, and in the evening it was like the appearance of fire over the tabernacle until morning." It was continuous – the cloud would cover it by day and the appearance of fire by night. The Lord was again demonstrating the fact that He was with His people. He has been with His people ever since He delivered them – He has birthed a people in Egypt and brought them out.

There would be something unnatural about any mother who would birth a child and then leave that child. When you give birth to a child, that is not the end – that is the beginning. You now have a life for which you must provide. You must nurture, love, and direct that child. Of course, God does the same. The Lord had birthed these people and brought them out of Egypt, and he would not then leave them on their own.

Praise the Lord that – when He saved us – He did not deliver us from our sin and then leave us on our own. He gave us His presence – He placed His Spirit within us! The presence of the cloud and the pillar of fire were a visual manifestation of the presence of God with His people, and it was with His people continually according to the scripture.

God literally "pitched His tent" (or tabernacle) among his people. Each Christmas – when we celebrate Advent – is a time when we recognize the glorious realities of what we call the incarnation. Emmanuel, God with us! As we celebrate Christmas, we are celebrating the fact that God stepped out of the glories and into our broken world, that God pitched His tent among us, that He sent His son into the world to seek and to save the lost.

When Jesus went away, He said to the disciples, "It is expedient for you that I go away. It's profitable for you that I go away because I will pray. The father and the father will send the Spirit, another comforter to come and to abide with you." God still dwells with His people, though He does not hover as a cloud or a pillar of fire that is glowing at night. Now, God manifests His presence by dwelling in the hearts and the lives of His people. Emmanuel, God with us!

I will confess that there is great physical comfort in a cloud by day and a pillar of fire by night. I can remember the days of family vacations to Florida or South Carolina. I am very fair-skinned, so – when everybody else was praying for sunshine – I was praying for clouds. You know what I am talking about if you have ever been out on a hot day working when a cloud comes and shields you from the blazing sun. What a comfort there is in the cloud protecting you from the heat! Where were the children of Israel? In the desert! The Lord is providing comfort by this cloud.

I watch a lot of the nature survival shows on television. One of the first things you must do when you set up your camp before nightfall is build a fire. There is something comforting in the darkness of the night about having a fire. For the people of Israel, the comfort they receive from the cloud by day in the desert was mirrored by the comfort they received at night from the pillar of fire – to be able to look out and see a visual reminder that the Lord was with them.

I believe this is the result of a supernatural divine act of God. This was not just any cloud, and this was not some special manifestation of nature. The Bible says that this cloud accompanied them for forty years throughout all their journeys – signifying the presence of God was with them. How wonderful, how awesome, that God dwells with his people! Are you glad that the Lord has promised to you and me that He would never leave us nor forsake us?

God said to Jacob in Genesis 28:15, "Behold, I am with you and I will keep you wherever you go, and I will bring you back to this land, for I will not leave you until I have done what I promised. Then Jacob woke from his sleep and said, Surely the Lord is in this place, and I did not know it."

God said to Joshua in Joshua 1:9, "Have I not commanded you? Be strong and courageous. Do not be frightened, and do not be dismayed, for the LORD your God is with you wherever you go."

David reminded Solomon of God's faithfulness in 1 Chronicles 28:20, "Then David said to Solomon his son, "Be strong and courageous and do it. Do not be afraid and do not be dismayed, for the LORD God, even my God, is with you. He will not leave you or forsake you, until all the work for the service of the house of the LORD is finished."

The Lord has promised repeatedly, "I will not leave you nor forsake you." Some may say those are all examples from the Old Testament, but the same God in the Old Testament is the God of the New Testament. The writer of Hebrews reminds us of this in Hebrews 13:5-6, "Keep your life free from love of money, and be content with what you have, for he has said, "I will never leave you nor forsake you. So we can confidently say, "The Lord is my helper; I will not fear; what can man do to me?"

Remember, God was faithful to these people even though they were rebellious, disobedient, grumbling, and complaining all the way. Still, the Lord was faithful to remain with them, and I find great comfort in that. I wish I could tell you that I never grumble and complain. I wish I could tell you that I always step out and move when the Lord says move. I wish I could tell you that I never lack faith and never have any rebellious spirit within me, but I want you to know that is not true.

I can tell you what is true – God will never leave you nor forsake you. The Lord is with us, but He does not promise us a journey without a storm. He does not promise us a journey without a trial. He does not promise us a journey without adversity. What he does promise is that he will be with us in the journey and the adversity and the trial and the storm.

Faith in God is not a foolish belief – it is a confidence based upon God's perfect record of keeping his promises. I hope you caught that because it is good. Faith is not a foolish belief, but it is a certainty. It is an assurance. It is a confidence that is based upon God's perfect record of keeping his promises. God has never broken one. He has never failed once. He has never let any of His promises go by the wayside.

The Lord provided His people with – not only His continual presence – but His continual guidance. The cloud was abiding over the tabernacle, but it did not always stay there. There were occasions when the cloud would move, and they would set out at the command of the Lord. The Lord is leading and guiding His people. Just like you and I, these people needed guidance and direction – they had never been to the Promised Land.

If you go back five hundred years, their ancestors had made the journey to Canaan and back, but these people had been slaves in Egypt. They did not know the way to the Promised Land because they had never been this way before. They desperately needed the direction of the Lord.

We desperately need the Lord to direct our path. I have never been this way before, and I do not know what tomorrow holds. I do not know what God has planned for us in the future, but I know we need to be listening for the voice of the shepherd. Are you glad that the shepherd leads the sheep?

In scripture, we could be called a lot of things, but we are called sheep. I would have rather been called lions or tigers or bears (oh my!), but we are called sheep. I think one of the reasons that God calls us sheep is because sheep are geographical morons – they are easily lost. They easily go astray, so sheep desperately need a shepherd. Do you have a shepherd guiding you?

You will be easily lost without the shepherd. You will easily go astray. You will get your head down – feeding upon green grass here and there – then look up and not know where you are. It is easy to go astray, so we need to be listening attentively to the voice of the shepherd. Do you know His voice? Are you listening for Him? The Bible says in John 10:1,

"Truly, truly, I say to you, he who does not enter the sheepfold by the door but climbs in some other way. That man is a thief and a robber, but he who enters by the door is the shepherd of the sheep to him, the gate keeper open. The sheep hear his voice and he calls his own sheep by name and he leads them out. And when he has brought out all of his own, he goes before them and the sheep follow him, for they know his voice."

Are you listening to the voice of the shepherd? Are you attentive? Are you staying up close to the shepherd? Following the Lord demands our full attention. The children of Israel had to be constantly watching – constantly aware of where the cloud was. It was not predictable – which is the thing that spoke to me most in this chapter.

No matter the time of day – whenever the cloud was lifted – they would set out.

There was nothing predictable about when the cloud would move. You could not get up in the morning and assume the cloud was going to move in just a few minutes because it was eight o'clock. You could not get up after being in one place for a week and know the cloud was going to move because it was a Monday. No, the cloud moved whenever the Lord moved the cloud.

It might be that you just got your camp set up and settled and the next morning the cloud is moving, and you have to pack up everything. You may get settled in a hard place and then you are there for a week or a month or a year. Has the Lord ever left you in a hard place for a week or a month or a year and it seems as though the Lord is not speaking? It seems the Lord is not moving, and sometimes watching and waiting become very difficult.

These people had to give their full attention. Have you found the ways of God mysterious in your journey? I can honestly say to you, I found it very perplexing. The ways of the Lord are not predictable. The ways of the Lord are mysterious beyond our comprehension. This is what the Psalmist says in Psalm 139:

"Oh, Lord, you have searched me and known me. You know, when I sit down and when I rise up, you discern my thoughts from afar. You search out my path and my lying down and are acquainted with all of my ways even before a word is on my tongue. Behold. Oh Lord, you know it all together. Listen, you hear me in behind and before you lay your hand upon me, then he says this such knowledge is too wonderful for me. It is high. I cannot attain it."

I think this is what Paul means when he wrote in Romans 11:33, "Oh, the depths of the riches and the wisdom and the knowledge of God. How unsearchable are his judgments and how inscrutable his ways for who has known the mind of the Lord or who has been his counselor?"

I ask again, have you often found the ways of the Lord mysterious? Have you often wondered why it was not more predictable? Have you ever wondered why God left you in a hard place for a month or a year? Have there been times when it seems like the voice of the Lord is silent and He is not moving in the direction that we expect?

Remember, His ways are higher than our ways. Every decision we make or judgment we render, we render with limited wisdom and understanding. We only know part of the impact of our decision – God knows at all. God knows how every decision will impact you, how will it impact your family, and how it will impact those around you. God knows all of the ramifications of every decision and every path that we take.

For that reason, it is wise to listen to the voice of the shepherd. It is wise to allow the Lord to direct your path, because if we go out leading our own way, it will usually be devastating. At best, it will be debilitating and dangerous, but it may be devastating. How better it is to listen to the voice of the shepherd! But following the Lord also demanded great faith.

Has the Lord ever called upon you to move when you are not ready to move? He is moving your cloud – leading you out – and you just got things settled. We are people that like to nest and to settle. That is why we have storage buildings in our backyards. That is why we have those pull-down stairs that we can climb up in the attic to store things we will never remember to find again.

We like to nest. We like to get rooted and grounded. My wife and I have a home in Maryville, Tennessee. We call that our home, but that is not our home. That is a temporary dwelling place. We nest there, we settled there, we put down a few roots there, but we are pilgrims and strangers. We need to always be ready to move when the Lord says move!

That is what the Lord is teaching His people. Has God ever led you somewhere where you thought maybe He had led you to a dead end or taken a wrong turn? I want you to know that the ways of the Lord are always right. They are always sure – even when it does not seem that way to us.

Have you noticed how easy it is to see the will of God looking backward and how hard it is to see the will of God looking forward? I look backwards, and it is like a light shining on it. It seems so clear when viewed through the lens of experience. It was the will of God for you to be born into the family that you have. It was the will of God for you to grow up in that home and for someone to share the gospel with you. It was the will of God, and you recognize it now. Looking into the future, however, we have a hard time distinguishing His will as His ways are mysterious and unpredictable to us. Rest assured, the same God who was guiding you in the past – that has proven to be right and steadfast and true – is the God who is going to lead you in the future.

Elizabeth Elliott wrote something wonderful when she said this, "Today is mine. Tomorrow is none of my business." Then, she expounded upon it, "If I peer anxiously into the fog of the future, I will strain my spiritual eyes so that I may not see clearly what is required of me today." That is good!

As a pastor, when somebody says they need to talk with you about the will of God for their life, they are most often wanting an answer to a particular decision they are about to make. They want to know the will of God about which job to take, which college to attend, who to marry, or something like that. The will of God, though, is not just about getting us from point A to point B – it is about the journey and the process. It is about God molding us and shaping us in that process.

Allow me to recommend another book to you. It is a small, old book written by Chuck Swindoll entitled "The Mystery of God's Will." It was published in 1999, so you may have a difficult time finding it, but it is a great one. In it, he addresses how the will of God is not about what job to take or what move to make – it is about becoming the person that God wants you to be.

God is in the process of molding us, shaping us, and forming us. He does it in the journey. The whole time He is moving us from point A to point B, it is not just about that – it is about becoming who God wants us to be in the journey. Life is a journey, not just a destination – and God is at work in your life. We are all a work in process, and none of us have arrived yet. Sadly, we can be very impatient with each other. Do not be hard on somebody because they are not where you are in the journey – be understanding. We are all in a different place in this journey, but God is at work.

God is with his people. God is guiding his people. Praise the Lord! He is at work in your life and in my life today.

LET THE JOURNEY CONTINUE

A mother in Indiana gave birth to a set of twins and they were born thirty minutes apart. Since the deliveries occurred around midnight, the twins were actually born on different days. It also happened to be New Year's Eve, so they were also born in different years. To really complicate things, it was at December 31, 2019 and January 1, 2020, so these twins were born in different decades. Try explaining that for the rest of your lives! Praise the Lord for their mother that it was only a thirty-minute delivery – as it sounds much, much longer.

The children of Israel probably felt the same way. Their journey probably seemed much longer than one year. In Numbers 10:11, we begin the second "section" of the book. The first thirteen months have been spent at Mount Sinai where the Lord has been giving them instruction – sharing the law with them. He has been giving them instruction concerning the building of the tabernacle – a dwelling for God among His people.

Now, the Lord is leading them forward from Mount Sinai as they make their way to the land that God had promised to give to their father Abraham. The journey now continues – a journey from Egypt to Mount Sinai becomes a journey from Mount Sinai to the promised land.

The sad part of the story is that these are some of the darkest days in the life of the nation of Israel. These days would be filled with grumbling and complaining and rebellion and disbelief as the Lord brings them to the very shores of that promised land where they – because of unbelief – refuse to enter. These are dark days for the nation of Israel.

The journey started out well, though. They begin following the Lord as He leads them forward and the cloud moves out – signifying that it is time to move. The Lord is leading His people forward.

Numbers 10:11-12, "In the second year, in the second month, on the twentieth day of the month, the cloud lifted from over the tabernacle of the testimony, and the people of Israel set out by stages from the wilderness of Sinai. And the cloud settled down in the wilderness of Paran. They set out for the first time at the command of the LORD by Moses".

These verses are very significant because they serve to remind us – lest we ever forget – that the stories we are reading are real historical narratives. They are not fiction or fairy tales. This is not a story about a land far, far away in some unknown time. It is story set in a real place and a real time with real people.

As we consider this text, we recognize that this not only is historically true and accurate – a historical narrative – but it is pinned down for us to teach us more than history. We read this historical narrative not just to learn about an ancient people and their travels through the Middle East, but we are reminded that these are the people that God has redeemed and that He is guiding them and leading them. These people foreshadow you and me as redeemed children of God. We are on a pilgrimage, too, and we desperately need the Lord as we look into the future.

Have you got it all figured out? Do you know what the future will hold for you? If so, you must certainly have greater vision than I do. I do not understand or even pretend to know everything that will take place in the future. What I do know – as one of His sheep that tends to wander – is I need to keep my eyes upon the Lord. I need to be listening to his voice as one of his sheep.

It is amazing to me – when I think about the people of Israel – how it is possible that these people we are reading about here had witnessed the greatest manifestation of the power and glory of God. They had witnessed God doing miraculous things. They had seen God work through the plagues to humiliate Pharaoh. They had seen God roll back the Red Sea as they walked across on dry ground. They had seen God provide manna from heaven. They had seen God provide water from a rock. They had seen God demonstrate his power and glory through signs and wonders over and over repeatedly. Yet this very generation would be the generation that would reject the same God that had redeemed them.

How is it possible that those who had seen God's faithfulness in such a miraculous way could ever turn away from him? This sad fact is true in our own day as well. May we not be a people that are always demanding something of God. May we not be a people that are always looking for signs and wonders. May we not be a people so shallow that we constantly demand that God prove himself to us. There are many that live that way – people who say, "if God would only _____ then I would believe." If God would only bring about this miracle, if God would heal this person, if God would fix this problem, if God would only do this and this, then I would believe.

God has nothing to prove to me. God has nothing to prove to you. Rather than seeking signs and wonders, may we be a people that trust Him for who He is – not for what he should do. May we just trust Him because of His nature and His character. Those that live by signs and wonders demonstrate that they have a shallow faith indeed. Jesus, in his teaching concerning the rich man and father Abraham in Luke 16, said this:

"I beg you, father, send them to my father's house, for I have five brothers so that they may warn them, lest they also come to this place of torment. But Abraham said they have Moses and the prophets let them hear them. And he said, No, Father Abraham, but if someone goes to them from the dead, they will repent. And he said to him, if they do not hear Moses and the prophets, neither will they be convinced if someone should rise from the dead."

Guess what? One did rise from the dead, and people still do not believe! Do you believe in the risen Son of God? I would recommend the book "Evidence That Demands a Verdict" by Josh McDowell if you are serious about seeking the truth and desire honest examination of the evidence.

God's steadfast love upon me all these years of my life is more than enough. If God should see fit to never answer another prayer or do another mighty act or deed in my life, I want you to know He is still God and He is worthy of our trust. I do not know what your situation is or what you may be up against, but trust God whether you see the signs and the miracles and the wonders or not. Just trust Him for who He is – for He is a God that loves you greatly.

I must remind you that those who have been saved are redeemed people. We have been bought with a price. Your life is not your own – you belong to God. If you have been born again this day, you are a redeemed people.

Now, let the journey continue. There are three things I want to draw your attention to and focus on.

Number one is: "We have a commander-in-chief leading us."

As the cloud began to move out, we might expect that there would have been a great deal of excitement among the people. Do you get excited before a trip or a journey? I find it very difficult to sleep the night before I am going to take a trip. Are you that way? I wake up several times in the night and look to make sure my alarm is still set.

If we get excited about a trip, imagine these people. They have been waiting for over a year at Mount Sinai, and finally, the time has come for them to head out as the cloud begins to move. It says the cloud was lifted from over the tabernacle of the testimony and the Sons of Israel set out on their journeys from the wilderness of Sinai. They moved out – it says in verse 13 – "according to the commandment of the Lord through Moses." When you look at these people, I want to remind you that God was leading them as an army into battle.

When you look at Numbers 10:14-27, you have a listing of each one of the tribes and the way they were to set out. Just notice with me verse 14, "The standard of the camp of the people of Judah set out first by their companies, and over their company was Nahshon the son of Amminadab."

Depending on what translation of the Bible that you have, it may say "armies," it may say "hosts," or it may say "companies," but it is all the same. It is the reminder to us that God has now organized the nation of Israel into companies and tribes that were a mighty army. God has taken a group of former slaves out of Egypt, redeemed them, and now set them in order. He has organized them in such a way that they are marching forward under the command of the commander-in-chief, God, as He is leading His people. God has set each one of them in their place.

In the opening chapters of the Book of Numbers, God numbered the people according to their age and ability to go out to battle. When you look at the verse 14, you find some words that remind us that this is indeed a mighty army that is marching forward, and it uses the word "standard." That standard is a banner or a flag. Each one of the tribes were marching according to their standard. Each tribe was marshaled under its chief and all their movements rallied around their own standard, their own banner. F.P. Meyer says, "For a whole year, Israel had sojourned under Sinai. They left Egypt an undisciplined crowd and they have now become a nation and a martial host."

Every tribe had its appointed place. If you do not learn anything else about the book of Numbers, I want you to learn the fact that God has an order for things. God has ordered the nation and appointed them where to camp, when to march, and how they were to march. When the cloud lifted, it was not mass chaos. It was not everyone suddenly going in all directions, because God had taught them. God had directed them and appointed a place for each of them – and everyone knew their place. Everyone was responsible to follow the command of the Lord and move out according to their place.

God is still a God of order. Would you agree the universe that God has created demonstrates God's order? In society and in culture, God desires order. Do you recognize that one of the realities that we are facing in our day is that Satan is doing everything that he can to disrupt and to distort and to pervert God's ordained order in every area of our lives? Do you see that?

The second thing in this passage I want you to see is: "Moses invited others to join them in the journey."

Numbers 10:29-32, "And Moses said to Hobab the son of Reuel the Midianite, Moses' father-in-law, "We are setting out for the place of which the LORD said, 'I will give it to you.' Come with us, and we will do good to you, for the LORD has promised good to Israel." But he said to him, "I will not go. I will depart to my own land and to my kindred." And he said, "Please do not leave us, for you know where we should camp in the wilderness, and you will serve as eyes for us. And if you do go with us, whatever good the LORD will do to us, the same will we do to you."

As I understand this family relationship, this is the brother-in-law of Moses (the son of his father-in-law Jethro). His father-in-law has been of great benefit and help to Moses. He has given him great counsel in the past. Jethro was a man God used to teach Moses many things. Now, Moses is inviting his brother-in-law to come along on the journey to this place that God has promised He is going to do good to us – and what God does to us, He will do to you. What a gracious invitation! Come along with us to the promised land.

This is a microcosm of God's plan for the church. God designed Israel to be a light to the nations. Israel is supposed to be a blessing to all people. Israel was supposed to be a people that would share the glory and the light of Jehovah God with all the nations. If you miss this fact, then you have misread your Bible. God desired to use the nation of Israel to be a light to the world.

We see that throughout all the Old Testament. We see God raising up a prophet by the name of Jonah and sending him to the Assyrians to preach the gospel. That whole city came to faith and were saved and spared. God was a God that wanted to use his people to be a blessing to others. We see that with the story of Ruth the Moabitess woman. In God's providence, He used her to be in the lineage of the Messiah. Jesus himself, in Luke 4, one of the things that He said that disturbed the Jewish leaders more than anything else was in verse 25-28:

"But in truth, I tell you, there were many widows in Israel in the days of Elijah, when the heavens were shut up three years and six months, and a great famine came over all the land, and Elijah was sent to none of them but only to Zarephath, in the land of Sidon, to a woman who was a widow. And there were many lepers in Israel in the time of the prophet Elisha, and none of them was cleansed, but only Naaman the Syrian." When they heard these things, all in the synagogue were filled with wrath."

What is Jesus saying here? He is saying God has always had a heart for the Gentiles – that God always desired to do good and to be merciful to them. How did this message go over? It says when they heard these things, all that were in the synagogue were filled with wrath and they rose up and they drove him out of town and brought him to the brow of the cliff of a hill in which their town was built so that they could throw him down off from the cliff, but passing through their midst, he went away.

What is God teaching us? God's plan is for those of us who are on this pilgrimage to invite as many as we can to come along with us. May God help us say to our brother-in-law, to say to our friends and our neighbors, to say to our coworkers, "come along with me."

God may not send us to India, but he may send us across the road. He may send you down to the next workstation. He might send you to another classroom. God wants the people who are on the journey to constantly be saying, "come."

The final point is: "The presence of God went before the children of Israel."

Numbers 10:33, "So they set out from the mount of the Lord three days journey. And the ark of the covenant of the Lord went before them three days; journey, to seek out a resting place for them."

Now, this was different and unusual. Normally, the traveling orders for the nation would involve the ark being right in the center. Most of the times of journey, the tribes set out with the priest and the tabernacle right in the middle so the priest carrying the ark was protected on every side. The ark was usually in the middle.

For the first three days of this journey, though, it says that the tabernacle went before them. This was the hardest part of the journey if you look at it geographically. This was a "No Man's Land." Their journey was one from a wilderness to a wilderness. Nothing easy about this, but our journey in this life is also from a wilderness to a wilderness.

If you are expecting heaven here on earth, you will be sadly disappointed. If you are expecting Utopia, if you are expecting a bed of roses, if you are expecting it to be easy, then the reality of life's disappointments will be crushing. We are living in a wilderness, and we are on a wilderness journey. We will arrive, but it will not be in this life. While we are here, we are going to be in the wilderness. Buckle up and keep your eye on the Lord. Make sure that you are close to Him. Make sure you are following Him because this journey is going to be difficult.

Praise the Lord that we have one that has gone before us! We are not journeying without a guide. We are journeying with that one that has blazed the trail before us. The fact of the matter is the Lord went before them a three-days' journey to find for them (I love this part) "a resting place."

Listen to what the Bible says in Hebrews 12:1-2: Therefore, since we are surrounded by so great a cloud of witnesses, let us also lay aside every weight, and sin which clings so closely, and let us run with endurance the race that is set before us, looking to Jesus, the founder and perfecter of our faith, who for the joy that was set before him endured the cross, despising the shame, and is seated at the right hand of the throne of God."

Praise the Lord that we have a "trailblazer!" That word there in verse 2 that is translated "author" can also be translated "pioneer." It means one that has gone before. It is the one who has blazed the trail. Listen, the journey that you and I are on may be difficult and rough, but Jesus has gone before us!

Fix your eyes upon Him.

LET THE GRUMBLING STOP

Did you ever take a road trip with your family when your children were little? If so, you can relate to the task of Moses. The Israelites began the journey in chapter 10, and we read, "they marched out according to the commandment of the Lord." They marched in the order that the Lord had designated for them, and I am certain there was much anticipation and excitement. The long-awaited journey was off to a good start!

Immediately, we come to chapter 11, and we are confronted with the reality that the people are now grumbling and complaining. "Let the journey start" and "let the grumbling stop" are often close together. Every parent understands this fact. The trip can be off to such a great start – you get to leave on time, the bags are packed, and everybody is happy in the back seat – and it is still not long until "let the journey begin" becomes "let the grumbling stop."

Quite often, we have heard those familiar phrases from the back seat, "are we there yet?" Followed a little bit later on from the backseat by, "stop touching me! Quit touching me!" You put your parental authority in gear, and you get the "touching" stopped only to hear, "he's looking at me! Make him stop looking at me!" Is it any wonder why this crowd in Numbers was called the "children" of Israel? Moses had a large congregation of spiritual infants – a traveling party of grumblers and complainers.

People often wonder when reading these passages what this story has to do with our story. These are ancient Israelites who are grumbling, and they could not possibly have any relationship to us modern, enlightened Americans today, could they? We would never be guilty of grumbling and complaining like these ancient people here in the book of Numbers, would we?

The reality is that we are all cut from the same cloth. Since the events of Genesis 3, we all have an Adam nature. We have a fallen nature with its proclivity toward discontentment. We have a proclivity toward grumbling and complaining. The people of Israel were just like that, and I have to say to you many times I am as well.

If I were to give you a piece of paper and ask you to write down the most grievous and serious of sins, I doubt complaining and grumbling would be on your list. It is not one of the "seven deadly sins," we might say. Is it really a sin to complain and grumble? Is it a serious issue? It may be like a fever – a symptom of something greater.

When we open Numbers 11, the first three verses give us a snapshot of what was going on among the people. This is a scene that it is replayed often in our own spiritual journey.

Numbers 11:1-3, "And the people complained in the hearing of the LORD about their misfortunes, and when the LORD heard it, his anger was kindled, and the fire of the LORD burned among them and consumed some outlying parts of the camp. Then the people cried out to Moses, and Moses prayed to the LORD, and the fire died down. So the name of that place was called Taberah, because the fire of the LORD burned among them."

How many times do we listen to the enemy and grow discontent with the Lord's provision? God is worthy of our praise because He is the sovereign God of this universe. He sustains not only the whole universe, but He is our sustainer as well. He sustains our life, and He provides all that we need. He was doing this for the children of Israel, but they were not satisfied. When we grumble and complain about our hardship, when we grumble and complain about the adversity in our life, when we grumble and complain because the journey is hard, we are just like these ancient people.

Such discontentment and grumbling are displeasing to the Lord because the Bible teaches us that all we have is a gift from him. Do we recognize this? We in America like to talk about pulling ourselves up by our bootstraps and being a self-made man, but the Biblical reality is, "everything we have is a gift from him." All that you have, God has given to you.

Considering it has "all" come from the good hand of God, what does it reveal when I begin to grumble and complain about what God has given to me? Who is the focus of my discontent? I am grumbling about the God – the sovereign God, the loving God – who has given to me everything that I have. We may think that grumbling and complaining are no big deal, but they are symptomatic of a much greater problem. Whenever we are consumed with discontentment, murmuring, grumbling, and a spirit of criticism, it is symptomatic of something going on in our heart.

As Americans, we are good at this. Are you amazed at how spoiled we have become? "First world problems" is an accurate phrase as we often grumble and complain about things that much of the world could never imagine. We grumble and complain because the line is moving too slow at the fast-food restaurant during our lunch hour. Do we not recognize that most of the people in the world are not driving a climate-controlled automobile through a line getting food handed to them out the window? Much of the world is living off beans and rice today with tomorrow's menu consisting of rice and beans. Here, we grow discontent with our choices of Mexican food, Italian food, Asian food, fast food, junk food, and on and on it goes.

It is easy for us to become grumblers and complainers – even with the bounty that the Lord has blessed us with. It may be symptomatic that we have forgotten the good hand of our God who has blessed us so richly. We have forgotten to be grateful for even the small things that the Lord has given to us. We must be careful that we do not allow the spirit of complaint to become a habit in our life.

I grew up in a little country church, and we had "Saturday night singings." They would invite quartets and groups to come in, and I can remember as a boy hearing a very unusual song about grumbling. I was able look it up and find it. It was in a songbook entitled, "Soul Inspiring Songs." Tell me if this inspires you.

"In every town and city, some people can be found who spend their time in grumbling at everything around, especially of holiness, some curious things they say, but if we're true to Jesus, we're sure to win the day.
Oh, we will work for Jesus and persecutions bear. And when we get to heaven, there'll be no grumblers there. But all will be converted and cleansed from every sin, no other kind of people will ever endure in.

Then the second verse, which surely must have been written by a discouraged pastor.

They grumble at the preaching, they grumble at the prayer, they grumble at the singing, they grumble everywhere.
They grumble if we speak to them, they grumble if we don't, they grumble if we visit them, they grumble if we won't.

Grumbling!

Let us glean a few things from this text.

First: "The redeemed people of God are often not content with Him or His provision."

Let us not forget who these Israelite people were – they were the people who cried out to God for deliverance from slavery in Egypt. They had seen the mighty acts of God. They had been delivered and were now being sustained by bread from heaven. The manna was given every morning for their provision. For forty long years in the wilderness, God faithfully sustained them. Great is His faithfulness!

They complained about their adversity because the journey was hard. The journey was hard, but the Lord was with them. They were not citizens of the wilderness – they were simply passing through the wilderness on the way to their homeland. Do you recognize that we too are pilgrims? It is easy to become so "rooted and grounded" in this present world that we forget we are only passing through.

They were complaining because the way was hard – often, I do likewise. They were complaining because the Lord's provision to them was not satisfying – often, I do likewise. God was miraculously providing all their needs – He is doing likewise for each of us today. Be grateful and thankful for the Lord's provision. The Lord sustained as many as perhaps two million people in the middle of the desert! I have had the privilege of traveling around that area and – without God's provision – no one could survive.

I heard about the little boy who in Sunday school kept learning about these children of Israel. He read about their complaining of hunger, so he raised his hand. He said, "I've got a question. Why didn't that Moses fella take them to McDonalds and get them all a Happy Meal?" Well, God gave them something better than a Happy Meal. God gave them bread from heaven, but they were not happy about it. God meets our needs, but not always our wants.

Sometimes we get confused between what is a genuine need and what is a want. There are a lot of things we might want, but we do not really and truly need. If we believe that God is all-knowing and sovereign, then we need to be satisfied when God says no to what we want and instead gives us what we need. It is hard sometimes, is it not? It is interesting that in Numbers 11:7-9, Moses, the author, gives us a description of manna.

"Now the manna was like coriander seed, and its appearance like that of bdellium. The people went about and gathered it and ground it in handmills or beat it in mortars and boiled it in pots and made cakes of it. And the taste of it was like the taste of cakes baked with oil. When the dew fell upon the camp in the night, the manna fell with it."

One English translation reads "the taste of it was like pastries." In other words, this provision was palatable – it was like a sweet pastry whenever they finished with it. When the dew fell on the ground at night, the manna would fall with it. It appears this manna was a very versatile, utilitarian source of sustenance. It could be boiled or ground into flour. There were so many various ways to fix it that it would be nice to find a Israelite cookbook with recipes for manna!

It was a pleasant food which God sent down to His people with the dew from heaven, but this sweet bread of heaven lacked the sharp and the savory and the sour which are stimulating to the palate. In other words, the people became bored with the provision of the Lord. The taste of Egypt was still upon their lips. They remembered their Egyptian diet of fish, melons, leeks, and garlic – a diet filled with variety that tantalized their palate. Now, they were being fed with bland manna every day!

I think there is a lesson here for us. An old Puritan writer wrote, "In this respect, the manna resembles the spiritual food supplied by the word of God, of which the sinful heart of man may also speedily become weary of and turn to the more spicy productions of the world." Did you get that? That is what is happening in American church today. Our spiritual appetites have grown tired of the Word of God, and we decide to spice things up a bit. We have decided to add some production – a spicy production of the world.

Guard yourself that you never lose your spiritual appetite for the word of God. It is the word of God that feeds our souls. It is the word of God that nourishes us. It is the word of God that comforts us. It is the word of God that instructs us. It is the word of God that first convicted us and brought us to faith in Christ. God forbid that we should ever be a people with such worldly appetites that we cannot simply gather if everything else is stripped away and we have nothing but the book – the Word of God. That should be enough.

Moses may have inserted (in verses 7-9) this short description to show us the iniquity of the people in their murmuring while they had such an adequate provision. It was all that they needed. It even had a great appearance – it appeared as "bedlam." The only other time that word is used is in the garden of Eden. It was beautiful in appearance, and it was more than adequate to meet their needs because it came from the good hand of God. The reference to the garden of Eden should serve to remind us that God provided for all of man's needs in the garden, yet Adam and Eve were discontent with everything the Lord provided and desired the forbidden fruit. We are all the sons of Adam!

It was easier to get the people out of Egypt than to get Egypt out of the people. By that I mean it was easier to get the people physically out of Egypt than to get the effects of Egypt out of the people. Before we judge them too harshly, is that not true of you and me? We are still in the world, and we often have appetites that are worldly and desire things that God has not provided for us. It is easy – even though we have been delivered from the world – to live according to its worldly desires.

The second thing in this text that speaks to me is: "Memories of the past can be vastly different than reality."

Numbers 11:5 is almost comical when you know the whole story. It says, "We remember the fish we ate in Egypt that cost nothing, the cucumbers, the melons, the leeks, the onions, and the garlic." Oh, how they forgot the reality of their affliction! When you read this verse, it seems as though they were having a picnic in Egypt. "It was so great when we were in Egypt, we had fish to eat free!" Was there free fish in Egypt?

If it was so great in Egypt, why did they cry to the Lord for deliverance? The Scriptures record the reality that they were an oppressed people being used by Pharaoh to enrich Egypt. The taskmaster's hand was heavy upon them. They were making bricks and laboring long days in the oppressive heat, so they cried unto the Lord for deliverance.

Now we find them remembering the past, and all they can think about was food – the variety of food they used to have. Is it not amazing how we remember the past better than it really was? When we were going through it, we were grumbling and complaining. Then twenty or thirty years later, we look back and say, "boy, those were the good old days." We did not think so at the time.

I have seen this phenomenon for myself. I have been a pastor for over thirty-five years – serving in three different churches. It is amazing how churches that I used to serve remember me differently now than they did when I was there. It truly amazes me at times – I am a really neat guy after I leave. Some of the very ones that were glad when I left their church later ask me to come back and do their funeral!

It is amazing how our minds distort the past to make it better than it really was, and so we are much like these people. Discontent with what God has given, desiring something more stimulating to our desires, and remembering the past – and our past life – better than it really was. What was the source of their grumbling? It was unbelief and ingratitude. What is at the heart of our discontent when we are grumbling against the Lord? Is it not much the same?

The Bible speaks about these people in Psalm 106:21-22, "They forgot God, their savior, who had done great things in Egypt. Wondrous works in the land of ham and awesome deeds by the Red Sea." It continues in verses 24-25, "Then they despised the pleasant land, having no faith in his promise. They murmured in their tents and did not obey the voice of the LORD."

Notice that final portion "having no faith in his promise...they murmured in their tents and did not obey the voice of the Lord." What was the source of their grumbling? They have forgotten God, they have no faith in his promise, and they are not obeying His word. God's people lacked the faith to trust Him to meet their needs, and too often, we are no different. We will trust Him when we can see it playing out our way. We can trust Him when we have a nest egg to fall back on safely. We can trust God if He provides all the answers ahead of time.

We need to be like the Apostle Paul who wrote in Philippians 4:11-12, "Not that I am speaking of being in need, for I have learned in whatever situation I am to be content. I know how to be brought low, and I know how to abound. In any and every circumstance, I have learned the secret of facing plenty and hunger, abundance and need."

Oh, that we would learn such a lesson! The writer of Hebrews says it like this in Hebrews 13:5, "Keep your life free from love of money, and be content with what you have, for he has said, "I will never leave you nor forsake you." In other words, if we have the Lord, we have all that we need.

It reminds me of the song that we often sing, "I'd rather have Jesus than silver and gold, I'd rather be his than have riches untold. I'd rather have Jesus than houses or land. I'd rather be led by his nail pierced hands, than to be the king of a vast domain and be held in sins, dread, sway. I'd rather have Jesus than anything this world affords today."

When we – as the people of God – live in godliness and contentment, the Bible says it is great gain. The Bible also says it is a great witness to a lost world. "Do all things without grumbling or disputing that you may be blameless and innocent children of God without blemish in the midst of a crooked and twisted generation among whom you shine as light in the world, holding fast to the word of life so that in the day of Christ I may be proud that I did not run in vain or labor in vain."

In contrast to a crooked and twisted generation, living a life of contentment without grumbling and disputing shines like a light. It is a bold witness that we have found in Christ all that we need and that we are satisfied in Him. When we are discontented, I truly believe it is because we have taken our eyes off the Lord.

Next, notice: "The spread of their grumbling went throughout the whole camp."

Here is a lesson we all need to learn – grumbling is a contagious disease. Do you know that grumbling, complaining, and criticizing can spread throughout a whole family of a whole congregation? The most dangerous diseases for society are highly contagious diseases. If COVID-19 has taught us anything, it is this reality. A contagion must be isolated so that it does not spread to others.

Our criticism and negativity can greatly influence others. Perhaps our negativity toward the Lord's provision may cause others to turn from the Lord. Whenever we get a spirit of criticism and complaint, whenever we see only the negative, it is not long before that is all that we see. We lose sight of the blessing and the good that the Lord is doing among us as the people of God.

Notice what the passage says. First, the grumbling started among the rabble on the outskirts. One translation calls them "riff-raff." Who were these riff-raff? Who were this rabble? Numbers 11:4, "Now the rabble that was among them had a strong craving. And the people of Israel also wept again and said, "Oh that we had meat to eat!"

This is the mixed multitude that has come along with Israel who are living on the outskirts of the camp. They are not really concerned about honoring God – they are traveling along with the children of Israel and gleaning the good that they can. They have no spiritual appetites, and this is where the grumbling started. It is often the case that in every congregation there are those that are on the fringes. There are those that are coming along with the crowd. There are those who have not truly been born again and do not truly have a spiritual appetite. Before long, they are grumbling and complaining – and their negativity about what "ought to be going on in the church" can infiltrate the whole congregation.

This is very applicable to where we are in the church today. If we are not careful, we will begin to design worship to tailor everything to respond to the needs of the rabble on the fringe. We may be tempted to change everything because of the grumbling of those who have no spiritual appetite that are truly not born again. I do not seek to offend anybody unnecessarily, but lost people should not be telling people how to worship King Jesus. The Bible should be telling us how we worship King Jesus – not polls, not opinions, not surveys – nothing but Scripture.

It may have started from the outskirts, but it did not stay there – it never does. The grumbling then was experienced privately within their tents. Deuteronomy 1:27 shares this about these people, "And you murmured in your tents and said, 'Because the LORD hated us he has brought us out of the land of Egypt, to give us into the hand of the Amorites, to destroy us."

They were grumbling and complaining about their hardships and about what the Lord was doing among them. They were doing this in their tents privately. As a pastor, I say to you and warn you to be very careful. Be very careful when you are having conversations in your home and speaking negatively about the church, about the music, about worship, about Sunday school, about the preaching, about whatever – because little ears are listening.

There are many people that are turned off from church because they grew up going to church listening to mom and dad talking negatively about the church all the time. Little ears are listening – they may be over in the corner playing somewhere, but they are listening. It is your house, and you can do what you see fit in it, but I want you to know the words coming from your lips are influencing the views that your children and your grandchildren are going to have.

The younger generation has a keen eye for identifying duplicity in the older generation. They see how we act at church and talk about how wonderful it is only to go home and sit around the kitchen table and criticize everything that happened. That is duplicity, and your children and grandchildren will see through the hypocrisy of it.

The people in Numbers began complaining in their tents, but it did not remain in the tents. Before long, it went throughout the whole camp and became public. So much so that in Numbers 11:10 it says, "Moses heard the people weeping throughout all of their clans (families), everyone at the doorway of his tent." What had started on the outskirts among the rabble and was then whispered inside the tents is now being vocalized throughout all of the camp.

The word has come to Moses, and that is the final point: "Grumbling affected even Moses – grumbling affects the leadership."

No leader is immune from the destructive nature of grumbling and criticism. In 1 Corinthians 4:1, Paul urged his readers to consider him a servant and steward. "This is how one should regard us, as servants of Christ and stewards of the mysteries of God."

The word that he used there for "servants" was not "doulos" the word that is usually translated servant. Paul uses a different word – it would be used to describe an "under-rower." You may have seen movies with old ships where there were slaves rowing in unison in the belly of the ship. Paul is saying, "I want you to know I am not the captain of the ship. I am an under-rower. I am down in the belly of the ship with my hands on the oars like the others, and we are rowing together."

When we are all in unison together – with our hands on the oars – following the command of our captain and working together, the ship will move forward. When we let go of the oars, though, it is easy to go from rowing the boat to rocking the boat. It can happen very quickly. We lose sight of who we are and what we are supposed to be doing. May God help all of us to be like the apostle Paul in the underbelly of this ship – listening to the command of our captain and rowing the boat together instead of rocking the boat.

Moses was affected by the criticism and complaining that he was hearing, and this was a man with whom God spoke face to face. A great leader – certainly one of the greatest leaders in all the Bible. Now, even Moses is grumbling and complaining himself to the Lord.

Numbers 11:11-15, "Moses said to the LORD, "Why have you dealt ill with your servant? And why have I not found favor in your sight, that you lay the burden of all this people on me? Did I conceive all this people? Did I give them birth, that you should say to me, 'Carry them in your bosom, as a nurse carries a nursing child,' to the land that you swore to give their fathers? Where am I to get meat to give to all this people? For they weep before me and say, 'Give us meat, that we may eat.' I am not able to carry all this people alone; the burden is too heavy for me. If you will treat me like this, kill me at once, if I find favor in your sight, that I may not see my wretchedness."

It is very easy for leaders to shift from seeing people as a blessing to seeing them as a burden. I pray that God would shield all of us in leadership so that we never look at the people God has given to us as a burden instead of a blessing. Allow me to make an open and honest confession here. There have been people in my ministry I would notice on aisle 3 in the grocery store, and so I lingered as long as possible on aisle 2. Just being brutally honest with you, but I knew – if I crossed their path – I would be having a long conversation about everything that was wrong at church.

May God spare us of that! Let us strive to see the good that God is doing and not the negative, He is a good God – no matter your present situation or hardship you are facing. I want you to know God is sovereign over it, and He loves you and He is providing for you as you walk through the journey. He said He would never leave you or forsake you.

You can take that to the bank!

Elders and the Idolatry of Israel

*(This chapter is contributed by Dr. T.J. Whitehead –
Associate Pastor of Students and Families at Broadway
Baptist Church. T.J. is married to his wife, Kayla and they
have one son, A.J. Pastor T.J. is a graduate of
the Southern Baptist Theological Seminary in Louisville,
Kentucky.)*

Introduction
In Numbers 1 – 30, the Lord deals with two seemingly
separate but certainly related things. The first is Moses'
heart and ministry. This leader of Israel has reached his
breaking point, and the Lord introduces another level of
support for Moses and the people – elders. The second
issue this passage addresses is the Lord's judgement on
the people for their idolatry.

As we head into this Passage, let us consider the occasion
that gave rise to the appointment of elders. I am going to
argue that this Passage serves a fundamental role in what
will become the church's polity or government. As such,
this Text has special relevance for God's corporate people
today.

Eldership of Israel
The Occasion for Elders

10 Moses heard the people weeping throughout their clans, everyone at the door of his tent. And the anger of the Lord blazed hotly, and Moses was displeased. 11 Moses said to the Lord, "Why have you dealt ill with your servant? And why have I not found favor in your sight, that you lay the burden of all this people on me? 12 Did I conceive all this people? Did I give them birth, that you should say to me, 'Carry them in your bosom, as a nurse carries a nursing child,' to the land that you swore to give their fathers? 13 Where am I to get meat to give to all this people? For they weep before me and say, 'Give us meat, that we may eat.' 14 I am not able to carry all this people alone; the burden is too heavy for me. 15 If you will treat me like this, kill me at once, if I find favor in your sight, that I may not see my wretchedness." - Numbers 11:10-14

Moses is at his breaking point. Moses is pleading with the Lord to kill him – anything to relieve this burden of leading the stubborn Israelites. This is a common thing for Moses that stems all the way back to Exodus chapters 5-6. The people gang up on Moses with their complaints, then Moses – a not-so-self-confident man – asks the Lord, "Why? Why have you placed this burden on me, Lord?" It appears there are several things that are contributing to this mentality.

For starters, part of Moses' struggle is self-inflicted. If you recall, he has a tendency to be self-reliant. His father-in-law Jethro pointed this out to him and advised him to appoint judges (Exodus 18:13-18).

The second influence on Moses' burnout is the weight of ministry. Moses' ministry is not an easy one. We all are entrusted with ministry and people whom the Lord wants us to serve. Everyone's ministry context is different. This is especially evident among pastoral ministries. There are various factors that influence us here (the amount of responsibility and expectation, the level of support one receives, etc.), but you will see some pastors burn out after a year or two while others are able to demonstrate great endurance. A lot of that has to do with one's ministry context. Some leaders – by their own doing or by the unrealistic expectations of those whom they are accountable to – are set up for failure. This appears to be Moses' story. He is trying to go at it alone, and the people around him are too self-centered to be considerate of what they are putting their leader through.

The third influence on Moses' burnout is specifically the people and their constant complaints. Simply recall the devastating effect complaining has on a people and its leadership. Needless to say, Moses is overwhelmed with a terrible ministry burden and trying to do what he cannot do alone. The Lord in His mercy answers Moses' cry by providing structure to the government and ministry of Israel.

Multiplicity of Elders in Jewish and Christian Traditions

16 Then the Lord said to Moses, "Gather for me seventy men of the elders of Israel, whom you know to be the elders of the people and officers over them, and bring them to the tent of meeting, and let them take their stand there with you. - Numbers 11:16

It is easy to miss how foundational this Passage is, but this Text contributes several elements to the government of Israel and even to what will later be the government (or polity) of the church. Many of the characteristics of eldership are rooted here in Numbers. First, consider the multiplicity of elders that is patterned in Judaic and Christian polity. The pattern of 70 elders reappears roughly 1200 years later in the translation of the Septuagint. Have you noticed – in the footnotes of your Bibles – the letters "LXX?" That is shorthand for the Septuagint (L = 50, X = 10; LXX = 50 + 10 +10 = 70).

In the 2nd and 3rd centuries before Christ, there was already a significant Jewish population in Alexandria, Egypt, many of whom grew up in Egypt – which at that time primarily spoke Greek. These Jews who could not speak or read the Hebrew Scriptures requested of the High Priest in Jerusalem that translators be sent down to translate the Hebrew Scriptures into Greek. As the tradition goes, seventy-two translators were sent down to translate the Hebrew Bible into Greek. This tradition is recorded in a 2nd century document called the Letter of Aristeas.

Elders also appear in the Sanhedrin. The Sanhedrin was a council that we find recorded in the Gospels and Acts comprised of 71 Jewish leaders. This almost certainly followed the pattern established in Numbers 11 for you have the High Priest representing Moses and 70 leaders underneath him representing the 70 elders appointed in the wilderness.

What is most significant for us is how the pattern of a multitude of elders is picked back up in church polity. Some people have in their minds that the early church was primitive and lacked any formal organization. They proclaim, "I don't like organized religion" as a way to excuse themselves from gathering on the Lord's Day, but the church has always been organized and structured. Christ dictated certain elements of church government while He was on the earth:

1.   Jesus sent out 70 of His disciples (Luke 10:1-23)
2.   He gave the church instructions on church discipline (Matthew 18)
3.   Then, after He ascended, He directed His church to form greater structure (1 Timothy 3)

When we find the Apostles planting churches in Acts, what do they immediately do? During Paul and Barnabas's first journey – after certain believers had matured in the infant congregations – they appointed them as elders:

21 When they had preached the gospel to that city and had made many disciples, they returned to Lystra and to Iconium and to Antioch, 22 strengthening the souls of the disciples, encouraging them to continue in the faith, and saying that through many tribulations we must enter the kingdom of God. 23 And when they had appointed elders for them in every church, with prayer and fasting they committed them to the Lord in whom they had believed.
-       Acts 14:21-23

"Elder" is synonymous with "pastor" and "overseer." It is the most frequent of the three terms used of this office. As it is, there were to be "elders in every church." Every church had multiple elders appointed. This ought to be the goal of every local church. I know there are some who struggle due to their size, but it is the Apostolic pattern of a church having multiple elders - this finds its basis here in Numbers 11.

The Complementarian Perspective
Before we consider the mode in which they were appointed as elders, I want to emphasize first the complementarian perspective for the office of elder that runs continuously through the Scriptures.

Complementarianism – the position held by the conservative Baptist Church – is the view that men and women are both created in the Image of God and therefore equal in value and worth, but God has assigned roles in both the home and the church that are specific to the genders. Men and women were made to complement one another. Think of 1 Corinthians 12. If everyone were an eye, where would the sense of hearing be; or if everyone were an ear, where would the sense of smell be? We work better for God's glory when we recognize the uniqueness in which we were made and express His Image in roles He has created for us. He is the Creator and He knows how we best function. Conforming to His design is how we will ultimately flourish.

In opposition to this Biblical teaching, egalitarianism is gaining momentum in our Southern Baptist Convention. It suggests that Scripture does not present a distinction in roles to men and women in the church or the home. There is a very influential figure encouraging a spirit of defiance to this clear Biblical teaching today – that is Beth Moore. She used to be a fantastic advocate of the complementarian perspective but has since changed her position. It is part of my duty as an elder to warn the flock when someone influential has gone off the rails.

Therefore, let me recommend to you a statement that was published in 1988 by the Council of Biblical Manhood and Womanhood known as the Danvers Statement. An excerpt from that statement reads:
"In the family, husbands should forsake harsh or selfish leadership and grow in love and care for their wives; wives should forsake resistance to their husbands' authority and grow in willing, joyful submission to their husbands' leadership (Eph 5:21-33; Col 3:18-19; Tit 2:3-5; 1 Pet 3:1-7).

In the church, redemption in Christ gives men and women an equal share in the blessings of salvation; nevertheless, some governing and teaching roles within the church are restricted to men (Gal 3:28; 1 Cor 11:2-16; 1 Tim 2:11-15)." From our text in Numbers, the Hebrew word for man – "iish" is restrictively masculine. The same is true of the Passages cited in the Danvers Statement.

The Congregation's Authority

With that said, what was the mode in which these elders were appointed in the context of wandering Israel? The first thing we can say is that these men were already recognized by the congregation to be elders. What I am emphasizing here is the responsibility and authority that is placed on the congregation to recognize those called by God to serve in an ordained office. The men selected to be elders were already recognized by the people as having a leadership authority and quality to them.

16 Then the Lord said to Moses, "Gather for me seventy men of the elders of Israel, whom you know to be the elders of the people and officers over them, and bring them to the tent of meeting, and let them take their stand there with you.
-        Numbers 11:16

While the people were in Egypt, there were elders among them (Exodus 3:16-18). In fact, for a single occasion prior to this, God had Moses select 70 of Israel's elders to go up the mountain with Moses when the Old Covenant was being given to the people of Israel (Exodus 24).

What does the congregation have to do with it? These were men that congregation had already recognized as elders and officers. They had an established position before the people. Likely, some of these men were holding the office of "judge" that Jethro advised Moses to establish when they were beginning their journeys in Exodus 18. Jethro laid down the following qualifications of these men: they must be able men, God-fearing, trustworthy, and hating of dishonest profit.

In the New Covenant, what can we say about the elders the Apostles appointed in every church? These elders were not simply appointed by the Apostles without the congregation's affirmation and confirmation. We see multiple instances where the congregation is involved in the confirmation of those who would hold a church office: First, the appointing of men to the ordained office of deacon rested in the congregation's authority. The Apostle's proposal for the congregation to appoint deacons to assist them in ministry work was confirmed by the congregation and the whole company chose men they considered qualified to hold the office of deacon (Acts 6: 3-5). Another example is the selecting and sending out of Paul and Barnabas was the Lord working through the congregation at Antioch (Acts 13:1-3).

Outside of the Biblical witness, we have an example from one of the earliest Christian writings outside the New Testament by an elder at the church of Rome – Clement – which interpreted the appointing of elders as something the apostles did "with the congruence of the whole church" (William Williams, Apostolical Church Polity , 537).

We learn from the Scriptures that the church has the ability to recognize the authority of Christ. We have the innate ability as a child of God to recognize the authority of Christ in His Word. Christ said, "My sheep hear my voice..." (John 10:27). Furthermore, we also have the innate ability as one indwelled by the Holy Spirit to recognizing the Spirit's anointing of someone. When the Spirit moves, we are able to recognize it. When the Apostles led the church in appointing deacons, they told them to select someone who was "full of the Spirit and wisdom" (Acts 6:3) – an indication of the church's ability (and responsibility) to recognize those whom the Spirit has led to fulfill such a purpose.

Those who are called by God to hold an office in His church – deacon and elder – are anointed by God to carry out that office. Without the Spirit's enablement, they would not be able to perform that unique ministry. It is your responsibility as the collected people of God to be aware of God's moving in the heart of a man that He is leading to such a role.

Elders are Filled with the Spirit
17 And I will come down and talk with you there. And I will take some of the Spirit that is on you and put it on them, and they shall bear the burden of the people with you, so that you may not bear it yourself alone.
-        Numbers 11:17

There are a few things that need to be addressed from this verse: first, the same Spirit of God that anointed Moses anointed the elders. Second, this particular anointing of God's Spirit for those leading God's people is also seen in the prophet Elijah's departure. For example, 2 Kings 2:15 states that the spirit of Elijah now rests on Elisha. There we see God anointing the next prophet with the gifts and qualifications for that office. Third, in the book of Acts – if you look at each time the Apostle Peter begins to preach immediately after Pentecost – Luke inserts the statement, "Peter – full of the Holy Spirit – said unto them..." The same is said of Stephen twice when he preaches the sermon that gets him killed. Why would the New Testament authors go out of their way to point this out? It is because there is a unique and special anointing on the one who brings the Word of God and who is to hold an office amongst God's people.

The purpose of God's anointing is so that the people would know that this is not merely a work of man, but of God. Consider Paul's recollection of his preaching amongst the Corinthians:

"And I came to you in weakness and in fear and in much trembling, and my speech and my message were not in plausible words of wisdom, but in demonstration of the Spirit and of power, so that your faith might not rest in the wisdom of men but in the power of God." (1 Corinthians 2:3-5)

The Spirit not only gifts elders and deacons for their ministries, but given the fact that all of God's people are indwelled by His Spirit to advance the gospel, the Spirit manifests different gifts in His people according to His will:

4 Now there are varieties of gifts, but the same Spirit; 5 and there are varieties of service, but the same Lord; 6 and there are varieties of activities, but it is the same God who empowers them all in everyone. 7 To each is given the manifestation of the Spirit for the common good. 8 For to one is given through the Spirit the utterance of wisdom, and to another the utterance of knowledge according to the same Spirit, 9 to another faith by the same Spirit, to another gifts of healing by the one Spirit, 10 to another the working of miracles, to another prophecy, to another the ability to distinguish between spirits, to another various kinds of tongues, to another the interpretation of tongues. 11 All these are empowered by one and the same Spirit, who apportions to each one individually as he wills." (1 Corinthians 12:4-11)
Cessation of Prophecy

Early in the church's history, the office of prophet existed alongside the office of Apostle. Acts 13 states that "In the church at Antioch there were prophets and teachers" (v. 1) In Ephesians 4:11 Paul says that the ascended Christ appointed some to be Apostles, prophets, evangelists, and pastor-teachers. However, there is a pattern in Scripture of the office of prophet – and its corresponding gifts to enable one to fulfill this office (1 Corinthians 12) – of cessation. That is, this office was not a permanent one that continued in perpetuity in the church like deacon and elder.

After the prophet Malachi, God stopped raising up prophets and His people took notice. You can look at Jewish literature in between the Old and New Testaments like the books of the Maccabees, and there you will see the people stating that there has not been a prophet since Malachi. Likewise, after God stopped giving Revelation in the New Covenant, the offices of Apostle and Prophet ceased to be.

Why would the office of Apostle cease? There was a definite amount of people who witnessed the risen Christ. This was the qualification of holding that office (Acts 1). Why would the office of prophet and its corresponding gifts cease? God's giving of Revelation ceased. Our Text in Numbers 11 appears to me to be the foundation of this pattern of cessation

24 So Moses went out and told the people the words of the Lord. And he gathered seventy men of the elders of the people and placed them around the tent. 25 Then the Lord came down in the cloud and spoke to him, and took some of the Spirit that was on him and put it on the seventy elders. And as soon as the Spirit rested on them, they prophesied. But they did not continue doing it. -Numbers 11:24-25

The Holy Spirit's coming and anointing is a powerful occasion. When it came to the saints at Pentecost, there was an immediate and powerful manifestation of unique gifts to authenticate the message the Apostles were preaching. Likewise, when the Spirit came upon these elders, there was a powerful display of prophesying so that the people may know that what the elders were saying were not "plausible words in wisdom, but demonstrations of the Spirit and of power." However, it did not remain. It was not meant to remain, and it was not because of a lack of faith that their prophesying ceased. People do not exercise these gifts at will – only when the Lord so chooses.

A Humble Ministry

There is a tendency when the Spirit of God brings about a work through His people for others to become jealous. This is true of God's people in general – hence Paul's words in 1 Corinthians 12 about the diversity of gifts ought not be something we become proud or jealous about. Rather, we ought to celebrate the diversity and see the beauty and necessity of the various gifts and the part each plays in the Body of Christ. This is also true of those who hold an office amongst God's people, in particular.

"26 Now two men remained in the camp, one named Eldad, and the other named Medad, and the Spirit rested on them. They were among those registered, but they had not gone out to the tent, and so they prophesied in the camp. 27 And a young man ran and told Moses, "Eldad and Medad are prophesying in the camp." 28 And Joshua the son of Nun, the assistant of Moses from his youth, said, "My lord Moses, stop them." 29 But Moses said to him, "Are you jealous for my sake? Would that all the Lord's people were prophets, that the Lord would put his Spirit on them!" 30 And Moses and the elders of Israel returned to the camp." (Numbers 11:26-30)

Humility comes easier knowing what has just come before – that it is the Spirit who works – enabling us to will and to work. Moses understood this was a work of the Spirit, and not only welcomed it, but wished God would put His Spirit on more men – despite what it would mean for his own ministry personality.

John the Baptist expresses this. God the Spirit anoints God the Son incarnate for His ministry, and He begins baptizing. John's disciples become concerned about more people going to Christ than John. John understands that the ministry he has been entrusted with is not to exalt himself, but Christ. So he says, "He must increase; I must decrease."

When factions arise in Corinth, and the people begin to say, "I follow Apollos;" "I follow Paul;" "I follow Peter," does Paul become jealous and try to convince the other two factions that they need to follow his ministry?

4 "What then is Apollos? What is Paul? Servants through whom you believed, as the Lord assigned to each. 6 I planted, Apollos watered, but God gave the growth. 7 So neither he who plants nor he who waters is anything, but only God who gives the growth." (1 Corinthians 3:5-7)

It was not about Paul or Apollos or Peter. It was and is about Christ. This is why this Spirit comes – to draw attention to Christ (John 15:26). When the Spirit came upon the elders in the camp, Moses knew it was a work of the same Spirit Who had anointed him. Whatever God has called us to and gifted us for, it is to make much of Christ. There is no room for jealousy in God's Kingdom.
 God has dealt with Moses's heart – and His people – in grace by the appointing of elders. Nevertheless, there is judgement coming for the people's idolatry, which is the second major emphasis of the Text.

Idolatry & Judgement
The Spirit directs us to Christ. He sets our heart's attention and affection on Christ, but idolatry is our heart's preoccupation with something other than Christ. In other words, idolatry usurps Christ's centrality.

The People's Idolatry
18 And say to the people, 'Consecrate yourselves for tomorrow, and you shall eat meat, for you have wept in the hearing of the Lord, saying, "Who will give us meat to eat? For it was better for us in Egypt." Therefore the Lord will give you meat, and you shall eat. 19 You shall not eat just one day, or two days, or five days, or ten days, or twenty days, 20 but a whole month, until it comes out at your nostrils and becomes loathsome to you, because you have rejected the Lord who is among you and have wept before him, saying, "Why did we come out of Egypt?"'
-        Numbers 11:18-20

I am arguing here that the people's complaining is nothing less than idolatry. Why do I say that?

First, because idolatry is subtle and pervasive. In verse 20, the Lord counts their complaining as "rejecting the Lord who is among you." The first two commandments are a condemnation of idolatry. This Passage reveals that idolatry is not just the explicit act of recognizing a false god or the worship of a physical engraving. No, idolatry can be a subtle thing – and it is pervasive. We are guilty of it all the time. As John Calvin said, the human heart is an idol-making factory.

Here are some litmus test questions that my Biblical counseling professor taught me that help unveil the subtle idols of the heart: Where does your mind go when you are on idle? What are your shower thoughts? When your mind is allowed to be free from daily tasks, where does it naturally drift to? This is where it should go:

"Blessed is the man
who walks not in the counsel of the wicked,
nor stands in the way of sinners,
nor sits in the seat of scoffers;
2 but his delight is in the law of the LORD,
and on his law he meditates day and night." (Psalm 1:1-2)

You and I have to be constantly disciplining our minds. As Paul says in Timothy, discipline yourself for godliness. Keep the Word of God with you so that you can meditate on it when your mind is idle so that you can discipline it to incline itself to God's Word. Parents, this is why Deuteronomy 6 says to talk about the Word with your children when you lie down and when you rise, when you are sitting at home and when you walk about the way. You are training their minds in the way they ought to go.

Here are some questions to ask yourself: What do you sacrifice for? You only have so much time – you cannot do everything that is before you. The sacrifices you make reveal your priorities. What do you sacrifice church for? If your budget is tight this week, what gets sacrificed? Your leisure expenses or your tithes? If you are wondering if something is an idol or not, ask these questions: Do I sin in order to get it? Do I sin when I do not get it? Does it consume me?

Idolatry is not just subtle – it is also irrational. There is an irrationality to sin. That is because God is rational, and sin is a deviation from the mind and will of God. Every time we give into our sin, we are trying to put back on the shackles which Christ freed us from. Why do we do that? It is irrational.

The Idol Consumes the Idolater

Let us look beginning at verse 18 again.

18 And say to the people, 'Consecrate yourselves for tomorrow, and you shall eat meat, for you have wept in the hearing of the Lord, saying, "Who will give us meat to eat? For it was better for us in Egypt." Therefore the Lord will give you meat, and you shall eat. 19 You shall not eat just one day, or two days, or five days, or ten days, or twenty days, 20 but a whole month, until it comes out at your nostrils and becomes loathsome to you, because you have rejected the Lord who is among you and have wept before him, saying, "Why did we come out of Egypt?"'21 But Moses said, "The people among whom I am number six hundred thousand on foot, and you have said, 'I will give them meat, that they may eat a whole month!' 22 Shall flocks and herds be slaughtered for them, and be enough for them? Or shall all the fish of the sea be gathered together for them, and be enough for them?" 23 And the Lord said to Moses, "Is the Lord's hand shortened? Now you shall see whether my word will come true for you or not."
- Numbers 11:18-23

Moses initially does not think this act of God is possible. Maybe God is exaggerating. But sure enough, God is able to bring about this judgement:

31 Then a wind from the Lord sprang up, and it brought quail from the sea and let them fall beside the camp, about a day's journey on this side and a day's journey on the other side, around the camp, and about two cubits[b] above the ground. 32 And the people rose all that day and all night and all the next day, and gathered the quail. Those who gathered least gathered ten homers.[c] And they spread them out for themselves all around the camp. 33 While the meat was yet between their teeth, before it was consumed, the anger of the Lord was kindled against the people, and the Lord struck down the people with a very great plague. 34 Therefore the name of that place was called Kibroth-hattaavah,[d] because there they buried the people who had the craving. 35 From Kibroth-hattaavah the people journeyed to Hazeroth, and they remained at Hazeroth.
- Numbers 11:31-35
What a disgusting image! This is to paint a picture in our minds of an ungrateful and pouty people who pitch a fit and cannot control their lust for their idol. This is what it looks like to the Lord when we forsake Him. As human beings who have yet to be freed from our fleshly bodies, we still have a proclivity to sin – a nature that we have to put to death daily. If we do not, our sin will sweep us away. It will carry us far off course before we come to our senses.

His sinful appetite carried the prodigal son far from home and brought him low before he woke up. The idolatry of Solomon led him to waste much of his life searching for meaning and satisfaction apart from God. What did he find after he saw each pursuit to the end? "It was vanity, vanity, a chasing after the wind."

Conclusion

I do not know what fleshly desire you are currently battling. All I know to do is say "wake up." Put your sin to death. Look to Christ. Your idols will only leave you empty and in despair. Christ will fulfill your every longing so lay your idols down and cling to Him.

If you do not know Christ, judgement is coming for you, idolater. The arm of the Lord is not too short. You will not escape His judgement. We are all born idolaters, but we do not have to remain that way. By God's grace, He rescues His children from their bondage and – in an act of Fatherly mercy – He even makes us sick of the things we once craved.

Surrender to Christ and be transformed from an idolater to a child of God.

FAITH OR SIGHT: HOW WILL YOU WALK?

People are people. How often have we read the stories of people in the Bible and somehow thought they were some "super" Christian and nothing like us at all? As we consider the Israelites and their exodus and wanderings, we need to recognize that they are very much like we are. There are many life lessons that we can learn by observing these ancient people and their experiences. They serve as a type or a foreshadowing of you and me?

Truth be told, we are more like them than we realize. As such, we do not simply have the story of an ancient people leaving Egypt on their way to the promised land, but we have the gospel illustrated before us. These things have been written so that we might learn from their example – they are written for our instruction. Their journey has brought them to the doorway of the promised land. It should be for them a time of great celebration. It should be for them a time of consummation – experiencing the fulfillment of all the promises that God had made to Abraham concerning this land. It should be a time of consecration where they consecrated themselves unto the Lord as they prepare to enter the promised land. Remember, these are the people that have seen God do mighty works and wonders repeatedly.

These are the people that were in Egypt when God demonstrated His might in the sending of the ten plagues. At the end of the plagues, there was no doubt who the Lord was! When He was finished with the gods of the Egyptians, all the peoples and nations could know that the God of Israel had delivered them.

Then He brought them out to the Red Sea. There they stand between a rock and a hard place. They stand with the sea before them, mountains beside them, and the Egyptian army closing in behind them. Once again, God demonstrates His might as He rolls back the Red Sea and allows his people to cross on dry ground. Safely on the other side, they turn and look behind them as God closes up the Red Sea and destroys the chariots and horses of this great land Egypt.

The list goes on as God provides food for them with manna coming down from heaven every day. God provides for them with water from a rock. They see the mountain of God at Mount Sinai on fire. They hear the voice of God as he gives to them his commandments and his laws while on the mountain. God also gives to Moses the design for the tabernacle. The God that had redeemed them would now be the God who dwells among them. As God pitches his tent through the form of the tabernacle in the camp amid his people. All the time, God was bringing them to a divine appointment – bringing them to the doorway of the promised land to give to them that which He had made a covenant with Abraham. It should have been a celebration!

What should have been a time of celebration ends up being a forty-year death march. Why? Because of their unbelief. They were at the doorway. It was time to claim the promises of God. Yet this generation was full of unbelief. This is a watershed moment for a whole generation of Israelites.

The New Testament writers understand the significance of this event. The Apostle Paul writing to the church at Corinth said in 1 Corinthians 10:11, "Now, these things happened to them as an example, but they were written down for our instruction on whom the end of the ages has come, therefore let anyone who thinks that he stands take heed lest he fall. Therefore, my beloved, flee from idolatry."

We are a people of a whole Bible. It is impossible to understand the meaning of the New Testament without some knowledge of the Old Testament. These stories are not just stories of an ancient people and an ancient land, but these are stories that are pinned down for our example – written down for our instruction. There is much that we can learn from these people and from this experience.

Namely: "Snatching defeat from the jaws of victory."

That is certainly one way to look at it. Another way to describe it would be drawing back from the promises of God. Certainly, there is a lesson that we need to learn from this story.

Let me begin by taking a moment to tell you a little bit about this promised land. Why is the land of Israel referred to as the "promised land?" It is not because it is some magical, mystical land. It is not like the beginning of some fairy tale "in a land far, far away." If you visit Israel, one of the things that will strike you is that – everywhere you step – you are encountering history and interacting with the Biblical narrative. This land is called the "promised land" because God made a covenant of promise with Abraham to give this land to him. It is a promise and a covenant that God kept.

This covenant is found several places in Scripture - first in Genesis 12:1-3, "Now the LORD said to Abram, "Go from your country and your kindred and your father's house to the land that I will show you. And I will make of you a great nation, and I will bless you and make your name great, so that you will be a blessing. I will bless those who bless you, and him who dishonors you I will curse, and in you all the families of the earth shall be blessed."

Before he ever left his home in Ur of the Chaldeans, the Lord spoke to Abraham and said, "I want you to know that I am going to take you to a land – a land that I will show you." Once Abram was in the land, God spoke to him again and established a covenant.

Genesis 15:15-21, "As for you, you shall go to your fathers in peace; you shall be buried in a good old age. And they shall come back here in the fourth generation, for the iniquity of the Amorites is not yet complete." When the sun had gone down and it was dark, behold, a smoking fire pot and a flaming torch passed between these pieces. On that day the LORD made a covenant with Abram, saying, "To your offspring I give this land, from the river of Egypt to the great river, the river Euphrates, the land of the Kenites, the Kenizzites, the Kadmonites, the Hittites, the Perizzites, the Rephaim, the Amorites, the Canaanites, the Girgashites and the Jebusites."

God reaffirmed this covenant to Isaac in Genesis 26:3, "Sojourn in this land, and I will be with you and will bless you, for to you and to your offspring I will give all these lands, and I will establish the oath that I swore to Abraham your father."

Then the Lord would confirm it to Jacob as recorded in Psalm 105:8-11, "He remembers his covenant forever, the word that he commanded, for a thousand generations, the covenant that he made with Abraham, his sworn promise to Isaac, which he confirmed to Jacob as a statute, to Israel as an everlasting covenant, saying, "To you I will give the land of Canaan as your portion for an inheritance."

During the burning bush experience, Moses hears these words in Exodus 3:7-8, "Then the LORD said, "I have surely seen the affliction of my people who are in Egypt and have heard their cry because of their taskmasters. I know their sufferings, and I have come down to deliver them out of the hand of the Egyptians and to bring them up out of that land to a good and broad land, a land flowing with milk and honey, to the place of the Canaanites, the Hittites, the Amorites, the Perizzites, the Hivites, and the Jebusites."

You may wonder why I take time to share all those references.

It is to remind us that our God is a covenant-keeping God.

Our God always keeps His promises! Even during those days when the children of Israel were in the bondage of Egypt, the covenant never left the heart and mind of God. God was going to bring His people into this land because He promised it to them. Is it not comforting to know – whatever situation you may be experiencing presently – God is faithful to keep His promises?

I want to affirm to you that the Lord is a faithful, covenant-keeping God. Everything in the Book that the Lord promises to His people, He will fulfill. I heard about a pastor that was visiting this little lady in the nursing home, and she asked him to read some scripture to her. He got her Bible off the nightstand and started to read. He noticed in the margin the letters "TP." As he looked at another margin – and all throughout her Bible – he found the letters "TP." He asked the lady, "I notice that you have marked in your Bible with these letters - "TP" – what does that stand for?" The lady replied, "Oh that means 'tried and proven.'"

Sometimes we forget about the steadfast faithfulness of the Lord. Sometimes we forget that every single promise He made in the Bible is indeed "tried and proven." Let us always remember – as the Lord reminds His people here in the Book of Numbers – He is a God who has made a covenant with them and He is faithful.

Those who have trusted Christ as Lord have entered into a covenant with God. It is the new covenant by the shed blood of our Lord and Savior Jesus Christ. He has not promised us a piece of property here on this earth, but He has promised us a place in heaven. If you are trusting in the Lord Jesus Christ, I want you to know He is going to keep His covenant. He is going to keep His promise. That is the reason Jesus could say, "all that the father has given to me, I have lost none." We can know that every one of God's children – one day – will make it safely home. Not based upon their faithfulness, but based upon the faithfulness of a powerful, loving, gracious, covenant-keeping God.

Now let us move on with the story of these Israelites as spies were to view the promised land. Numbers 13 begins with the account concerning a reconnaissance team that is sent to spy out the land in verses 1-2, "The LORD spoke to Moses, saying, "Send men to spy out the land of Canaan, which I am giving to the people of Israel. From each tribe of their fathers you shall send a man, every one a chief among them."

At first glance, it may appear that this was the Lord's idea, but – upon further reading – it seems that this was the people's idea. God was permitting it, but it was the people's idea. Listen to Moses as he recounts this experience in Deuteronomy 1:19-23:

"Then we set out from Horeb and went through all that great and terrifying wilderness that you saw, on the way to the hill country of the Amorites, as the LORD our God commanded us. And we came to Kadesh-barnea. And I said to you, 'You have come to the hill country of the Amorites, which the LORD our God is giving us. See, the LORD your God has set the land before you. Go up, take possession, as the LORD, the God of your fathers, has told you. Do not fear or be dismayed.' Then all of you came near me and said, 'Let us send men before us, that they may explore the land for us and bring us word again of the way by which we must go up and the cities into which we shall come.' The thing seemed good to me, and I took twelve men from you, one man from each tribe."

Hindsight is always 20/20. As Moses recounts this experience, I assure you he wishes he had a "do-over." The sending of the spies may have seemed the right thing at the time, but it turned out to be the source of great trouble. Have you ever experienced that in your spiritual journey? Yeah, me too!

The spy strategy only served to reveal what was in their hearts. We might applaud the military strategy of the people, yet it was unbelief that motivated their desire to see the land and who dwelled there. Alexander McLarens writes as follows, "A comparison with Deuteronomy 1:22 shows that the project of sending the spies originated in the people's fear at the near prospect of fighting which they had known to be impending ever since they left Egypt."

Robert Hawker wrote in his Poor Man's Commentary, "It appears as if the idea of sending men to search the land had originated in the Lords appointment, whereas by comparing this scripture with what is said there, we discover that it was fear and unbelief of the children of Israel and that they doubt that they had God's promises that first suggested in them the thought and then the Lord, as if in a gracious accommodation to the weakness of his people, permitted the thing. And had the spies been faithful and true to what they beheld of the promised land and had brought back a good report, all might still have been."

I think the reality is – whether this is the "perfect" will of God or the "permissive" will of God – He uses this to reveal what was in the hearts of the people. Does God not still do that many times? God many times bring us to a place to expose the unbelief, doubts, and fears in our very life. The Lord permitted or allowed this, but the Lord knew what was in their hearts.

By the way – as you read through the Book of Numbers – it is not very hard to see what was in their hearts. They consistently grumbled and complained – even though the Lord was providing for all their needs. They consistently remembered their past life in Egypt as some wonderful experience and forgot about the sorrows and taskmasters that they had in Egypt. Their hearts were full of unbelief, and the Lord uses this experience to expose that unbelief.

Has God ever brought you to a place of testing only to reveal that you were not nearly as prepared as you thought you were? I remember days in school when I thought I was prepared for the test – only to find out when I received my grade back that I was not nearly as prepared as I thought. It is at the time of the testing that we find out whether we are as prepared as we should be.

I remember one of the very first discipleship training courses that I ever took. It was the course, "Experiencing God" by Henry Blackaby. Many of you may have taken that course, especially if you grew up Sothern Baptist. In that course, Blackaby talks about a "crisis of belief" – a time when you come to a decision point or fork in the road. What will you do? Will you trust God for what He has said He would do? Would you trust God for what you know about His character? Will you walk by faith or will you walk by sight?

The spies gave an evil report – a report that lacked faith. What they saw in the land should have served to affirm their faith in God. Everything God had said about the land was true, but the majority of the spies lacked the faith to trust in the Lord's promises. The Bible says – whenever they came back to give their report – ten out of the twelve said, "There is no way! There is no way that we can enter this land. This land is full of giants and full of cities that are well fortified. This land is a land that devours its inhabitants."

The Bible says they gave a bad or an evil report to all the people. I think it is worth noting that the majority is not always right. Have you found that to be true? I know we live in America, and we really love democracy, but I want you to know that the majority is not always right. Sometimes the majority lacks the faith, sometimes the majority are blinded by unbelief, or sometimes the majority does not know anything about the Lord and what the Lord can do.

These unbelieving spies did two things.

First, they magnified the enemy.

They looked at the enemy and they said, "No way! We are grasshoppers and they are giants. They are much bigger and stronger than we are." They were right to the extent that "they could not" do it, but God could. F.B. Meyer writes, "Israel thought more of their enemies and their difficulties than the right hand of the most high God."

I would share with you that there have been many times that I have been right there and allowed the enemy to look much bigger than it really was. What is the giant that you are up against? Maybe you are facing a situation and it looks hopeless. Maybe it is a medical prognosis, maybe it is a family situation, or maybe it is a financial issue. You may be up against something and it looks just like a giant – like there is no way that you will be able to overcome this. I have found the more I focus upon the problem, the bigger the problem gets. What we must do is introduce our problem or situation to the Lord. When we take our giant problem and place it before the greatness and glory of our Omnipotent God, it does not seem nearly as gigantic.

Secondly, the unbelieving spies minimized the Lord.

They did report that all the Lord had told them was true, but they make no mention whatsoever of the Lord himself in their recommendation. They totally left the Lord out of the equation. As a Christ follower, when you begin to leave the Lord out of the equation, you will only get what you can do – not what the Lord can do. I have seen what man can do. It might impress other men, but it does not impress God. Do you long to see the Lord do something that only the Lord can do? He can do that in your situation.

William Carey – the father of the modern mission's movement – has this great quote, "Expect great things from God and attempt great things for God." This was written by a man who left Great Britain and went to Calcutta in 1793. He went there and devoted himself to translating the scriptures and then opening schools teaching the children how to read. How could Carey – in such a primitive time and place – make such a lasting impact? He expected great things from God, therefore he attempted great things for God.

Caleb and Joshua, on the other hand, did just the opposite of their fellow spies as they minimized the enemies and maximized the Lord.

They put the Lord into their equation and knew – since God was with them – He would give them the land regardless of the size of the enemy. If the Lord is with us, does it really matter who is against us? Is it not true that you plus the Lord equals a majority? Greater is he that is in you than he that is in the world! We need to magnify the Lord for He is faithful. He is going to do everything that He has promised. All the promises of the Lord are "tried and proven."

Hebrews 11:1, "Now faith is the assurance of things hoped for, the conviction of things not seen." He goes on in that chapter to say, "without faith, it is impossible to please him." Has the Lord demonstrated Himself faithful to you in the past? If He has, will He not be faithful in the future? The Bible says He never changes. He is the same yesterday, today, and forever.

Allow His steadfast faithfulness in the past to give you confidence to attempt great things for the Lord in the future.

UNBELIEF BREEDS REBELLION

Every great drama is filled with twists and turns – those unexpected as well as those anticipated. Every great drama is filled with heroes and villains, and so it is in the Divine narrative of Holy Scripture. Every great painting is made up of not only the bright light hues, but also the dark hues. At this point in Numbers, we arrive at one of the darkest hues in the painting of Israel's redemptive story.

The very people God had made a covenant with – the same people whom God delivered from the bondage of the taskmasters in Egypt – have now rebelled against Him. The very people whom God provided for by causing manna to fall from heaven and water from the rock – the same people whom God led by a cloud at day and a pillar of fire at night – have now turned against God and refused to obey him.

Is it not tragic? Is it not sad? The very people who have been the beneficiaries of such grace, provision, and faithfulness from God prove unfaithful to him at the moment of truth. Certainly, this was the lowest point in the history of this generation. Because of their unbelief, rebellion, and grumbling against the Lord, a whole generation of people will die in the wilderness. They would see the blessed promised land, but they forfeited the blessing.

It is amazing how many times when we study Old Testament narratives that we paint ourselves in the picture – typically in a very positive light. We look at the story of David and Goliath and imagine we would be like David when we would really be like the Israelites who are shuddering on the sidelines.

When we look at this narrative, let us not forget that unbelief can cause us to sometimes speak out against the Lord or to harbor feelings of resentment against the very God who has redeemed us. As we look at this narrative, let us draw out a few things. Notice that they mourned – the people mourned and wept all night. It says in Numbers 14:1 that the whole congregation lifted their voices and they cried, and the people wept that night.

The children of Israel had been confronted with two reports regarding the promised land. Twelve spies had been sent out (one spy representing each one of the tribes of the twelve children of Israel), and now they have returned. They went to view the land for forty days. They traversed the land from the north to the south. They went from the wilderness of Zin to the hill country. They even brought back some of the fruit of this land. They saw everything that the Lord had said was true. The Lord said, "This is a land that flows with milk and honey, a land of springs and fountains. This is a land that I promise to give to you. And it will be a land where I will sustain you. This is my promise to you."

They went and viewed the land and all of the spies saw the same things, but ten of them looked with eyes of unbelief. It was only two spies – Joshua and Caleb – that added God into the equation. Now, it was time to give the report and ten spies stood up and said, "Yes, indeed, the land is prosperous. Yes, indeed, the fruit and the produce are abundant." But they went on to say, "But the land will never be ours for the people in this land are giants. They are much larger than us and the cities of this land are walled cities and they are well fortified. And there is no way that this land will ever be our land."

The news of that report spread throughout the whole camp. By the evening, all the people of the congregation of Israel were mourning and weeping, and they wept throughout the night. If you had been in the vicinity that evening, you would have heard the weeping, wailing, and mourning that was going on throughout all the camp as they believed this report of unbelief.

However, as we have stated earlier, the majority is not always right. This may be the report of the majority, but it was a report that lacked faith. It was a report that left God out of the equation. According to what Moses would write later in Deuteronomy 1:28, "it caused the heart of the people to melt." The people were full of discouragement, and they were thrown into despair.

These ten spies were chosen from among the people, and what was a reality in their heart was also a reality in the heart of the people. What we find here is that these spies had a lack of faith. They were not depending upon the Lord, but they represented a people who were also a people of unbelief. What was true in their hearts was true also on behalf of the whole nation.

Now, the whole nation is weeping and mourning because of the report of these men. Israel wept that night upon hearing that the enemies in Canaan were formidable. They wept that night because they heard reports that the cities were well fortified. While there were many reasons why they may have mourned, I believe these three are certainly among them:

First, "They mourned because God had not made it easy for them."

They looked at the land and they saw enemies, giants, and well-fortified cities. To conquer this land would be a difficult endeavor – involving great hardships and struggle. Many times, we are just like the children of Israel. Have you ever come to the place in your life where you begin to mourn and despair because the way has gotten hard? When adversity, trouble, and sorrow come upon you, may I remind you of something? The Lord never said it would be easy!

We live in the day where we like things easy and comfortable. We do not like adversity, hardship, or suffering. However, Jesus never said that the way of the Christian would be easy. He did not say that it would be marked by a lack of adversity. In fact, Jesus said just the opposite. He said, "In this world, you will have tribulation." You can mark it down. No one will get through this life without a measure of adversity and tribulation. The Lord did not say, "Follow me and it will be easy." He says, "Take up your cross and follow me." While Jesus never promised it would be easy, He did promise to be with us. The Lord will be with us as we go through adversity and hardship.

This is proven repeatedly throughout the Holy Scriptures. Remember Joseph? I think we can agree Joseph's life was anything but easy. He was rejected by his brothers, thrown in a pit, and sold into slavery. Once in Egypt, he is falsely accused and placed in the prison. Does that sound easy to you? Does that sound like a life lived on a bed of roses? It sounds more like a lot of thorns to me.

Joseph's life was a hard one, yet repeatedly we read, "but the Lord was with Joseph." Even his master saw the evidence that the Lord was with Joseph and caused all that he did to prosper. Joseph may have felt alone at times, but he was never alone. You and I may feel alone sometimes, but the Lord is with His children in all their adversity and trouble.

If you are thinking that life is going to be easy, I need to introduce you to the word "reality." The reality is this life is not going to be easy but is going to be full of challenges. If you are a child of God, though, the other word I have for you is "hope." We have hope for the Lord is with us.

Second, "The nation mourned because they doubted God's love and provision."

Yes, the way can grow difficult, and often it grows mundane. They got bored! They got tired of the manna which the Lord provided. They would have liked to have some pizza for a change. Perhaps some chocolate cake would be nice, but God kept giving them this bread from heaven. You know what that manna was doing? It was sustaining them. God was providing for them. Is God not providing for us as well? It may not always be chocolate cake, but it meets our needs.

The people said the Lord has brought us out here to die in the wilderness. Recently, I was able to lead a group on a trip to Israel. We drove from the southernmost part of Israel north through the wilderness of Zin. This is the area where God sustained two million people for forty years. As we drove through this area, it appeared to me that it would be difficult to keep a goat alive in this barren wilderness.

Manna may have lacked the savory, salty flavors of Egypt, but it was more than sufficient to keep them from starving. They got bored with the provision of God. Being bored with God's provision is the source of many troubles. How often has a husband or wife gotten in a great deal of trouble because of boredom?

May we never question or doubt the love and provision of our faithful God. In the moment of adversity, the enemy will come and whisper in your ear, "If God loved you, why did this happen? If God really cared for you, why this medical report? If God really loved you, why this lay off at the plant? If God really loved you, why this rebellious child? Why this strained relationship?"

I want you to always know that God is faithful, and that God loves you. We may doubt many things, but we should never doubt how much God loves us. If God freely gave us His Son, will He not also give us all we need? If we ever doubt his love for us, look at the cross and be reminded of the love of God that He gave His only begotten Son. His love never changes – it is enduring and everlasting. His character is not in flux, but it is steadfast, faithful, and true.

Lastly, "The nation mourned because they had unmet expectations."

Many times, what brings us to a place of despair are unmet expectations. I can attest that many of our expectations are not Biblical expectations. We often have expectations that cannot be met in the reality of this imperfect broken world. We imagine and dream of a perfect world where everything is fair, but that is not the present world in which we live. What happens when our expectations are denied? We become disillusioned, we despair, and we grieve the loss of our dream. The Bible says in Proverbs 13:12, "Hope deferred makes the heart sick". Some translations render it, "a dream deferred that makes the heart sick."

I believe this was true for the children of Israel, and so they mourned. Not only did they mourn, but also the people grumbled. That should not take us by surprise, should it? These people have been grumbling ever since they left Egypt. If you want to do a good study, read through your Bible, and highlight every time you see "grumbling, complaining, or murmuring." It may be translated differently across translations, but it is all the same – discontentment, frustration, aggravation, and just basic lack of satisfaction with who God is and what He is doing.

So, we find the people grumbling yet again, and they grumble against Moses and Aaron. They finally come to the place – after complaining about Moses and Aaron and their leadership for a long time – where even the families of Moses turn against him and join with the people in deciding to follow him no longer. They desired to appoint a new leader and go back, because things were "so much better in Egypt" after all.

They wanted a new leader, but not only were they grumbling against Moses and Aaron – they were grumbling against the Lord. You see, this plan was not a plan from Moses. This was God's plan. Moses and Aaron were simply tools in the Master's hands. Not only were they grumbling against Moses and Aaron, but they were upset with the Lord, and they spoke against the Lord.

The Bible says, "And all the people of Israel grumbled against Moses and Aaron. The whole congregation said to them, 'Would that we had died in the land of Egypt! Or would that we had died in this wilderness! Why is the LORD bringing us into this land, to fall by the sword? Our wives and our little ones will become a prey. Would it not be better for us to go back to Egypt?' And they said to one another, 'Let us choose a leader and go back to Egypt.'"

Notice that they said, "Why is the Lord bringing us into this land to fall by the sword and our wives and our little ones will become plunder? Would it not be better for us to return to Egypt?" The people are blaming the Lord for a defeat that has not even happened yet! They are anticipating failure. They are looking down the road and building up a "what if" scenario. Do you ever do that? Do you ever live in that world with the endless road of "what ifs?"

They directly accused the almighty with the sin and evil of plotting the murder of them, their wives, and their children. May I inject something here? Being angry with God may be an experience we go through from time to time but be very careful how you express your anger. I have heard therapists say that it is good therapy when you are angry with God to go ahead and vent and "let it all out" and "tell God what you think about Him." You may feel better after the experience, but I want you to be warned – when we speak thus about God, we have sinned.

Now, I am not saying it is not okay when you have questions. I think it is quite appropriate – with the right attitude – to come before your heavenly father with all the respect and reverence you can muster and ask those questions. "Dear father, why? I do not understand this. I do not know why this is going on." That approach is very different than pointing your finger at God in anger, blaming, and making charges against Him. God has never done anything to hurt you or to wrong you. God has never sinned against His people. Has God ever sinned against you? Has God ever wronged you? The answer is no.

Therefore, we must blame somebody, right? We do that – play the blame game. It is our fallen nature, and it can be traced all the way back to the garden of Eden. When God came to hold man accountable for his sin, Adam said, "You know, it is not my fault. It is the woman's fault." Then he moved beyond that and said, "As I think about it, Lord, it is the woman you gave me." Adam tried to shift the blame onto God.

Be very careful when you blame God. Fear and unbelief can lead us to grumble, complain, and even rebel against the Lord and His will for our lives. When you find those early signs of doubt and unbelief creeping in, choose to – in the words of the great theologian Barney Fife – "Nip it. Nip it in the bud."

Remember that our God is providing for our needs. We may grow tired of the manna, but it sustains and grows us. The worldly taste and appetite of Egypt may still be tempting us, but allow the good, wholesome things of the Lord to satisfy you. God loves and provides for His own!

THE HIGH COST OF UNBELIEF

There is a cost – a price tag – attached to every decision. For the ancient Israelites, their unbelief would carry a hefty price. God had heard their cry for deliverance while they were slaves in Egypt, and He had brought them out. God sustained them in their journey and brought them to the doorway of the promised land. Unfortunately, the people listened to the report of the spies rather than the promise of the Lord and refused to enter.

Twelve spies were sent to view the land, and ten came back and gave an evil report to the people. It was an evil report because it was a report that lacked faith in God. They focused upon the enemies within the land rather than the God dwelling among them. The spies said that the land was too well fortified and that the inhabitants were giants. There was no way they could take this land. Because of their report, the heart of the people melted, and the nation mourned and wept and refused to enter. They stood in a place of unbelief and they refused to trust and obey all that the Lord has promised to them.

The Bible is filled with dark chapters telling of unbelief, rebellion, and disobedience, and Numbers 14 is one of those. Genesis 3 is such a dark chapter in the Bible also. Understanding the dark threads – those dark chapters in human history – is vitally important to understanding our present situation.

In Genesis, we discover that God created Adam and Eve and placed them in a perfect garden environment. God provided all they would ever need with only one stipulation – only one thing forbidden – yet they chose to disobey and rebel against their creator. In Genesis 3, God came down and pronounced judgment upon this act of treason and rebellion. It is indeed a dark chapter. It is a chapter that cast a long shadow over all human history. The reason why the world is in the mess that it is in can be traced all the way back to Genesis 3 and the rebellion that took place in the garden.

There was another very dark chapter in the Bible – Genesis 6. The Bible says that man's heart was only evil continually and God brought about a cataclysmic judgment. He brought judgment in the form of a universal worldwide flood. It is in that context, however, that we find the very first mention of the word grace. Noah found grace in the eyes of the Lord. Judgment mingled with grace – this is what we find in our story of Israel's unbelief. Praise the Lord for grace and mercy.

Let me remind us today of the seriousness of the sin of unbelief.

If I had given you a piece of paper and asked you to list the most hideous, terrible sins, probably no one would have listed the sin of unbelief. Usually when we list those sins, we list them based upon the consequences that they have between human beings. We would list sins such as murder, rape, or other crimes against humanity as being most serious, and they are indeed serious. However, I would assert that the sin of unbelief is the most serious of all sins. The sin of unbelief is the fountain from which many other sins spring forth. If you look back to the beginning – in the garden of Eden – you will find unbelief was the first sin. It was a serious sin for it was expressed against the God that created all.

Whenever we live our lives with unbelief, we diminish the very sovereignty and power of God. We also call into question the honesty and the truth of God whenever we fail to believe Him and take God at His Word. What we are conveying when we fail to trust God is either we do not believe that God is sovereign and powerful enough to do what He has said or that we believe that God is not trustworthy.

Unbelief is a great sin against God. When Jesus was talking in the upper room about the promise of the Holy Spirit, He said that the Holy Spirit would come and would convict of sin, righteousness, and the judgment. Then He goes on to say, "and of sin, because you refuse to believe in me".

It is indeed the sin of unbelief that condemns men and women, boy and girls, to eternal separation from God. Unbelief is indeed a grievous and terrible sin. The writer of Hebrews recognized that it is unbelief that caused the people to be on the unable to enter the promised land in Hebrews 3:19, "So we see that they were unable to enter because of unbelief".

They were not able to enter the fruitful land that the Lord had promised to them. Jude says it like this, "Now I want to remind you, although you fully once knew it, that Jesus, who saved the people out of the land of Egypt afterward destroyed those who did not believe."

The Apostle Paul, in writing to the church at Rome, would remind them that the casting off the nation of Israel – the fact that those branches were broken off and Gentiles were grafted in – was a result of their unbelief. Romans 11:19 reads, "Then will you say branches were broken off so that I might be grafted in? That is true. They were broken off because of their unbelief. But you stand fast through faith, so do not become proud, but fear. For if God did not spare the natural branches, neither will he spare you."

Why are these verses in the Bible? To remind us of the seriousness of unbelief, the seriousness of doubting what God has said, and the seriousness of not believing God. John Broadus was the second president of the Southern Baptist Seminary and a great scholar, and he wrote, "They did not believe the clear promise of God's blessing that had been so amply attested. But they did believe they exaggerated reports of difficulty." He goes on to say, "Men are ready to believe what falls in with their feelings or their carnal fears while they are slow to believe what God has spoken."

It is very easy for us – when times of testing come – to believe what lines up with our feelings and fears rather than the facts of the word of God. God had made a promise that He was going to give this land to these people, yet they chose to live in unbelief.

Those in our world today that refuse to believe what God has said concerning His son are abiding under the condemnation of God, because they refuse to believe the truth about who the Lord Jesus is. The Bible says in John 3:17, "For God did not send his son into the world to condemn the world, but in order that the world might be saved through him, whoever believes in him is not condemned. But whoever does not believe is condemned already because he has not believed in the name of the only son of God."

As we think about these ancient people and their unbelief, we need to recognize that unbelief of any kind is a serious matter. Ultimately, it is unbelief that causes men, women, boys, and girls to be abiding under the wrath and condemnation of God. It does not say condemnation somewhere in the future, but rather condemnation now.

The Scripture also declares that there is now no condemnation to those who are in Christ Jesus. The issue of condemnation or no condemnation is unbelief or belief. Have you put your trust in the Lord Jesus Christ? Are you abiding in unbelief? Do you receive the word of God and what God has testified concerning his Son – the Lord Jesus Christ?

If you do not, then why not trust God today? The wonderful reality is all of us at one time were abiding under that condemnation and then then we believed and trusted Christ. The Lord granted to us the ability to see the beauties of our Christ, and we cried out to him and received mercy and forgiveness. What He has done for countless others, He will do for You.

In addition, we should see that the mercy of the Lord does not negate the consequences of sin.

We like to believe that all we must do is say "I'm sorry," and everything is made right. I remember one of my grandsons went through a period when he was younger when he was not-so-nice to his older brother and would get into trouble for it. He went through a phase where he just automatically responded, "I'm sorry, I'm sorry!" Now, I am not so sure he was always sorry, but he thought this would keep him from being punished. We are often like that, too, hoping by quickly acknowledging that we are sorry that the consequences will go away. Sometimes we are just like that with God, are we not?

However, sin has consequences that often do not go away easily. God is merciful but also holy and just. There is a line out there that we must not cross. You may remember such a line from your own childhood. I knew when I was growing up that I had reached that line when my mother employed all three of my names – Robert Anthony Collins! I was usually just "Tony," but times like those were apparently the only reason my mother gave me three names when I was born.

Like disobedient children, Israel had crossed the line with God. The Lord said, "Moses, you step aside. I will destroy these people and I will build from you a great nation, one greater than these people." Then Moses got on his face before the Lord and said, "Lord, if you do this, all the other nations, they will hear of it and they will say that it's because you were unable to bring them into that. Your name and your reputation is more important than mine, Lord. So, I want you to be gracious to these people because it is your reputation. It is your name that is on the line. You are the one who brought them out of the land. You have sustained them, Lord, remember your covenant".

Because of the prayer of Moses, the Lord now pardons these people. When He pardoned them, though, it did not mean that all was good. It did not mean there would not be consequences to their rebellion and unbelief. God is merciful, yet He is also holy. Many people want a God that is all love and no holiness. That image of god is an idol created in the mind of man – not the God of the Bible. Yes, God is merciful, God is long-suffering, but He is also holy. God's glory is of ultimate concern. God said, "All the earth is going to be filled with my glory." God is going to receive glory either through grace or through wrath.

There are over seven billion people on this planet. Out of those seven billion people, there is a redeemed humanity who have experienced the amazing, awesome, redeeming grace of God. We who are redeemed will – throughout all of eternity – bring glory to God as examples of His grace and mercy. If you are saved, you are a trophy of God's grace! A million years from now, God will still be pointing to you and me saying, "Oh, look, there is another shining example of my grace and mercy."

Conversely, for all of those who reject God's Son and who will not believe the testimony that God has given concerning his Son, God will receive glory from them as well. For throughout all of eternity, they will be examples of God's justice, God's holiness, and God's wrath. Every person God has created is going to bring him glory. God will receive glory either through grace or through wrath.

I pray that each of you will turn to the Lord and understand what a fearful thing that it is to fall into the hands of a living God. There are people today who only focus upon the love of God – our culture, our society, and "prosperity gospel" preachers. All they want to focus on is the blessing and the goodness and the love and the grace. Yes, praise the Lord for that, but know for those that reject him, stand in opposition to Him, and defy Him, the wrath of God is a fearful thing. The Scriptures declare, "the Lord, your God is a consuming fire, a jealous God."

Any notion that God is "so loving" that in the day of judgment He is going to just "kinda lift up the fence and let everybody slide on into heaven" is nowhere in the nature, character, or attributes of God. The holiness of God will be maintained for eternity.

Additionally, God's judgment is sometimes swift and startling.

Notice what the Bible says in Numbers 14:36, "As for the men whom the Lord sent to spy out the land who returned and made all of the congregation grumble against him by bringing a bad report concerning the land, even those men who brought out the very bad report of the land died by a plague before the Lord."

Swift, startling judgment upon these men who were the leaders from the tribes of the nation with greater responsibility. They caused the heart of the people to melt by giving an evil report, and the Bible says that God killed them by a plague. Sometimes in the Bible, God acts in ways to demonstrate the seriousness of the situation. Sometimes, God acts in ways to make an example of a situation. We recognize that there are times in the Bible where his judgment is swift and shocking.

Nadab and Abihu – the sons of Aaron – offered strange fire and the Lord killed them. Ananias and Sapphire lied about an offering in Acts 5, and they died on the spot. Are you glad God did not continue that process for dishonesty? However, if God continued to strike down liars where they stood, the political process would get a lot easier.

The writer of Hebrews declares in Hebrews 10:31, "It is a fearful thing to fall into the hands of a living God." Most often, the judgment of God is more of a process. God is going to judge this entire nation, and his judgment is giving them the very thing they said they wanted. These people – when they were standing at the door of the promised land – cried out to the Lord saying, "It would have been better for us had we died in the wilderness." God said, "Okay, if that is what you want." God's judgment upon them was that their corpses would fall in the wilderness. Judgment was going to come, but it was going to come through a process of forty years – one year for every day that they spied out the land.

When I look at what God is doing in our world today, it seems as though we are living out Romans 1. It appears America – as a nation, culture, and society – is a living commentary of Romans 1 where basically God's judgment is giving them their heart's desire. God "gives them over" is what the Bible says.

Romans 1:21-28, "For although they knew God, they did not honor him as God or give thanks to him, but they became futile in their thinking, and their foolish hearts were darkened. Claiming to be wise, they became fools, and exchanged the glory of the immortal God for images resembling mortal man and birds and animals and creeping things. Therefore, God gave them up in the lusts of their hearts to impurity, to the dishonoring of their bodies among themselves, because they exchanged the truth about God for a lie and worshiped and served the creature rather than the Creator, who is blessed forever! Amen. For this reason, God gave them up to dishonorable passions. For their women exchanged natural relations for those that are contrary to nature; and the men likewise gave up natural relations with women and were consumed with passion for one another, men committing shameless acts with men and receiving in themselves the due penalty for their error. And since they did not see fit to acknowledge God, God gave them up to a debased mind to do what ought not to be done."

Finally, we should recognize that the sin of one generation affects the future of the next.

Have you ever talked with someone that you really love in trying to hold them accountable? You are trying to talk to them about something that is in their life that is concerning to you, and they say, "Well, it is my life, and what I do does not affect anybody else." Well, I want us all to know that is a lie because God has built it so that our lives do affect one another.

The influences you allow in your life are going to affect others, too – maybe it will affect your children or your grandchildren. What we find in this text is that the unbelief of one generation causes the next generation to have to spend forty years of hardship in the wilderness. Yes, they will eventually inherit the land, but not for forty more years. Notice what the Lord says about this in Numbers 14:31: "But your little ones, who you said would become a prey, I will bring in, and they shall know the land that you have rejected."

It is never good when God throws our words back at us. I do not want my children or grandchildren to have to spend time in the wilderness because of my unbelief or unfaithfulness. What we do now impacts the next generation. There are few things that break my heart more as a pastor than dealing with brokenness in families. Counseling little children who are having to deal with adult problems when they should be playing. They should not have thoughts on their minds about parental addictions and all that brokenness getting dumped on them as little children.

It is all over our culture. It is all over our communities. We recognize that little children are having to deal with grown-up stuff, and it breaks my heart! We need to recognize that God has called us to walk as men and women of faith, to trust him, and to live that out before our children because God forbid they should have to suffer time in the wilderness because of our unbelief. I have used the reminder many times that what you might do in moderation, your children or grandchildren may do in excess. Indeed, I think we need to take our decision-making seriously, because what one generation does will affect the future generation.

If there is a bright spot in all of this, it is the faithfulness of two men. God rewarded Joshua and Caleb. The jeweler knows how best to present the diamond. He brings out the blank canvas and then he puts that diamond on it. Against the backdrop of that blank canvas, that diamond looks more beautiful than ever. Amid the darkness of unbelief, rebellion, rejection, and judgment, there is a bright, shining diamond – actually, there are two of them. They are Joshua and Caleb – the two spies that brought back a report that was full of faith. They pleaded with the people not to rebel against the Lord, and God rewarded their faithfulness. They would spend forty years in the wilderness, too, yet they would inherit the promised land. The only two of that entire generation that were going to enter in were Joshua and Caleb. God is faithful to keep His covenant – even during man's unfaithfulness.

The Lord will be faithful to us as well. He has promised us a land – heaven will surely be ours!

COPING WITH A CRISIS

Crisis management is a very important lesson to learn in this wilderness journey we find ourselves on. It is always good to be prepared in a crisis. Make sure you have extra water when you plan a long hike, extra gas when you are driving cross country, and extra food when you are going on a trip. Can you really prepare for every crisis, though?

No one can predict or anticipate every possible coming crisis – otherwise it would not become a crisis. No one in the early days of 2020 could have ever imagined the chaos, division, and confusion that would come into our world through an invisible enemy called the coronavirus. No one could imagine two years later we would still be dealing with Covid. This virus created a crisis in our world; however, it was not the first such crisis nor will it be the last.

We have been walking with Moses and the children of Israel as they experienced one crisis after another. Moses probably spent more time in crisis management than any other leader in all the Word of God. He has gone from rebellion to grumbling back to rebellion again. Moses lived through unprecedented times!

It is amazing to hear the words we have used during the coronavirus that we had never used before. "Unprecedented" is a word that gets thrown around more than ever these days. "Global pandemic" is another, and we had never heard of "social distancing" until 2020. One of the most humorous things I saw on social media was a picture of Pharaoh the King of Egypt with the caption "And you call this a plague? Where are the locusts, the flies, and the frogs?" When we consider what Moses had experienced, the term "unprecedented" takes on new meaning.

Moses was a man who had experienced a great deal of crisis and now we find him in Numbers 20 with yet another crisis. We could almost use the term "déjà vu" because it seems as though we have been here before. When we read Numbers 20, immediately our mind goes back to the experience recorded in Exodus 17. There, you have the people of Israel – on the very beginning of their journey – coming to a place where they grumble and complain about having no water to drink. God instructs Moses to strike the rock and from the rock God gave life giving water.

Now, we are at the end of the journey, and they are getting close to entering the promised land. The former generation characterized by unbelief has died away, a new generation now has taken their place, and they are getting ready to enter. Guess what? They come to a hard place, and they rebel just like their parents before them. They grumble and complain to the Lord. This time, however, the Lord instructs Moses not to strike the rock but rather to speak to the rock, and that the Lord would provide life-giving water.

We see that Moses does not follow the command of the Lord. Rather than speaking to the rock, Moses strikes the rock. Because of this disobedience, the Lord brings judgment on him, and he is not allowed to lead the people into the promised land. He and Aaron both will be restricted from being able to enter the Promised Land.

Here, we see: "Grief causes us to react in very uncharacteristic ways."

For us to understand the situation Moses experienced, we need to reflect on a few things the text reveals. The scene opens with the death of Miriam and it closes with the death of Aaron. I believe all scripture is inspired by God, and therefore, every detail given to us by God has a purpose and is shared for a reason. In Numbers 20:1, we simply have a reference to the death of Miriam. There is not a lot of explanation or exposition to be given – simply stated, "Miriam died there and was buried there."

Then, when we come to the last two verses of the chapter we read about Aaron's death. This was not an easy time for Moses or the people of Israel. We could almost outline the chapter as, "death, disobedience, and more death." We have this occasion of Moses striking the rock bookended by the reference of his older sister dying in verse one and his brother dying in the last two verses. I believe that this is very significant.

I believe God is giving us a little bit of insight into what was going on in the life of this man Moses – a man who is having a personal crisis, a family crisis, and a national crisis. Moses is a man who is dealing with grief and loss. He is dealing with the loss of his older sister. Think for a moment with me concerning the journey that they – Moses, Aaron, and Miriam – have been on.

This wilderness trio has gone from Egypt out into the wilderness to the very door of the promised land and then turned away and wandered around in the desert for the last forty years. They have experienced the divine hand of God – in bringing about a people that were no people out of the land of Egypt – guiding them all along the way. They had witnessed many miracles together. They had a great deal of experience together. They had walked together in this journey of life.

Now, consider some of the memories. I guarantee you there were good ones and some of them not-so-good. Just like our lives, when we reflect and think about those that we have journeyed with for a long time, there are some experiences that are very positive and some that are negative – so it must have been with the death of Miriam. It stirred up a lot of things in this man Moses that I believe may have contributed to what he does in this passage of scripture.

To our point that grief can cause us to react in very uncharacteristic ways, I believe Moses was a man at this time having a personal crisis while grieving the loss of his sister, grieving the loss of his brother, and grieving the people's continual rebellion against him and the Lord. Moses probably thought he was back at square one. After all this time, the new generation was complaining and grumbling just like the former generation. I would say that Moses was a man who was struggling with grief and loss.

As we each deal with grief our emotions can manifest in many forms. We may vent unexpectedly, we may withdraw from those we love, or we may struggle with feelings of guilt and remorse. Have you ever faced that difficult struggle? Thinking things like, "If I had only gotten that person to the doctor early" or "if I had only done this or that things would have been different." We can build up all kinds of scenarios. We can have all kinds of guilt when it comes to personal loss. I believe grief is one of the heaviest loads for anyone to carry, and Moses was just a man.

Memories, though, are truly a gift. Miriam was the one who stood by the River Nile to see what would happen to the baby in the basket. Miriam was the one that arranged for Moses' mother to nurse him. Miriam was one who would sing praises to the Lord for His mighty acts, but also the one who would rebel against Moses and become a leper for a period. There was a lot of experience that probably went through the mind of Moses whenever his older sister passed away.

While the opening of the chapter is the death of Miriam, the close of the chapter is the death of Aaron. Aaron was the elder brother of Moses – three years older and his right-hand man. In the burning bush experience – when Moses gave all the excuses why he was not the man for the job – God graciously gave him Aaron as a mouthpiece. Like Miriam, Aaron was certainly not perfect, but he was with Moses all along the journey.

Moses was a man experiencing a personal crisis and a family crisis. He was also experiencing a national crisis. This new generation seem to be repeating the sins of their parents. An interesting thing in the Bible is the record of many times when we see the proclivities toward a particular sin being repeated from one generation to another. I think that is what we are seeing here.

The apple has not fallen very far from the tree, and this generation responds just like the one before them. When they come to time of testing, they rebel and cry out against the Lord. When faced with a lack of water and resources, rather than crying out to the Lord for help and trusting in the Lord, they respond like their forefathers some forty years before them by complaining and turning against Moses.

May I ask if you ever struggle with those tendencies that cause you to distrust the good hand of God? We all have personal tendencies and weaknesses that can lead us astray. We need to recognize that all of us have personal proclivities toward particular weaknesses and sins. When we recognize those, we must be willing to make war against them. We need to confess them for what they truly are – sins.

I know that there are those tendencies in my life, and I wish I could say I have overcome all of them, but I have not. I recognize that they are sinful tendencies in my life and if I should list them for you, that would be all you could see. It would be like pointing to a blemish or spot on a wall – once you notice it, that is all you can see. Have you ever been there? You get done painting a room, and you think you have done well until somebody points out that one little place that you missed. After it is pointed out, you cannot see anything else but that spot. If I told you all my proclivities and my weaknesses, they would be easy to spot, but perhaps that is all you would ever see again. We all have them.

In this passage, we see not only that sinful tendency among the people, but it also reveals the sinful tendency in their leader. Moses is a man that we would characteristically describe as a very "meek" man. He may be the meekest man to ever live as he remained a very humble individual despite his close interaction with God. He is not a sinless or perfect man, though, and he also has some proclivities toward sin.

Moses also has some personal weaknesses in his life. He sometimes allowed his anger and his self-reliance to cause him to stumble. It was a much younger Moses that once killed an Egyptian and hid him in the sand. Because of that, he had to flee from Egypt and spent the next forty years on the backside of the desert taking care of his father-in-law's sheep. If there is a proclivity in the life of Moses, it is a tendency for him to allow his anger to get the best of him. You have this new generation of the people sinning against the Lord and Moses allowing his past anger to rule him – a true recipe for disaster.

Notice what the Bible says about their sin – as three things are detailed.

First, "they belittle the wrath of God." In Numbers 20:3, we read, "And the people quarreled with Moses and said, "Would that we had perished when our brothers perished before the LORD!" Now, who are they talking about? They are talking about those that God took out in a swift act of judgment. They said it would have been if they had been destroyed by the wrath of God in a swift act of judgment than to be the people that are starving to death in the wilderness. They were belittling the wrath of God. May I suggest you never make light of the wrath of God. I am glad that Jesus Christ absorbed the wrath of God on the cross because we cannot absorb it. The wrath of God is more than any of us can ever endure. Praise the Lord that Jesus took our wrath upon himself! Consumed with their physical hunger, this new generation said it would have been better to have been judged and have the Earth swallow them up than to be starving to death.

Secondly, "they minimize the power of God." In Numbers 20:4, they said, "Why have you brought the assembly of the LORD into this wilderness, that we should die here, both we and our cattle? In other words, they had forgotten the mighty hand of God. They had forgotten how God rolled back the Red Sea. They had forgotten how God had provided time and time and time again.

Finally, "they despise the provision of God." Notice what it says in Numbers 20:5, "And why have you made us come up out of Egypt to bring us to this evil place? It is no place for grain or figs or vines or pomegranates, and there is no water to drink." How have they been sustained for forty years? It has not been through grains and figs and pomegranates because they have been in the wilderness.

If you have ever visited that part of the land, you know what a wilderness is. There is nothing but rock and sand. How did God provide? How did God sustain these people? The provision of manna was not a one-time experience. It was an "all the time" experience. It was not just manna to eat for a week – God provided manna for them for all forty years that they were in the wilderness. They would never have been able to be sustained in that barren land except for the provision of God.

Now, they are despising the very provision of God – that manna that God gave to sustain their lives and provide them strength and sustenance to live in that wilderness. God provided for his people every single day throughout all their journey. He was faithful to His people, and He still is! I love the song that reminds us of this truth, "Great Is Thy Faithfulness."

"Great is Thy faithfulness, " O God my Father,
There is no shadow of turning with Thee;
Thou changest not, Thy compassions, they fail not
As Thou hast been Thou forever wilt be.
"Great is Thy faithfulness!" "Great is Thy faithfulness!"
Morning by morning new mercies I see;
All I have needed Thy hand hath provided—
"Great is Thy faithfulness, " Lord, unto me!

The scene then moves to Moses, and the climax is reached when he strikes the rock – the great sin that would keep Moses out of the promised land. Sometimes we may read this and think it unfair of God. After all, Moses was in a period of grief and crisis. This whole experience may seem uncharacteristic for Moses as well as uncharacteristic of God. It appears Moses made one misstep and God then forbade him to enter the promised land, but there is much more going on than meets the eye – that is usually the case.

Notice what the Bible says in Numbers 20:6, "Then Moses and Aaron went from the presence of the assembly to the entrance of the tent of meeting and fell on their faces. And the glory of the LORD appeared to them." That was a good thing to do, right? They ran to the house of God and did the same thing they had done so many times before – they fell on their faces before the Lord. If there is one thing that we need to learn from this, it is that we need to turn to the Lord in a time of crisis. We need to run to the presence of the Lord and get on our faces before him. The great blight upon America is a great blight of unrepentant sin. We need a spiritual awakening. Political answers will not solve it and economic stimulus is not going to fix it. We must get on our faces before God, cry out in repentance, and pray that God would be merciful and gracious to us.

Moses and Aaron's initial response was appropriate, but what happened next was not. The Lord spoke in Numbers 20:8, ""Take the staff, and assemble the congregation, you and Aaron your brother, and tell the rock before their eyes to yield its water. So you shall bring water out of the rock for them and give drink to the congregation and their cattle."

So far, so good. They are on their face before the Lord, and He comes and speaks and gives you instruction. Now comes the problem that Moses and Aaron do not follow the instruction and the command of the Lord. It says in Numbers 20:9-11:

collinsTony

"And Moses took the staff from before the LORD, as he commanded him. Then Moses and Aaron gathered the assembly together before the rock, and he said to them, "Hear now, you rebels: shall we bring water for you out of this rock?" And Moses lifted up his hand and struck the rock with his staff twice, and water came out abundantly, and the congregation drank, and their livestock."

God's instruction was clear and precise; however, this is where Moses goes rogue. This was not what God had instructed or said to Moses. This is now Moses speaking – not the Lord! "'Listen now, you rebels, shall we bring forth water for you out of this rock,' then Moses lifted up his hand and he struck the rock twice with the rod, and water came forth abundantly and the congregation and their beasts drank."

Here we see the grace of God as He provided for the people even though the leadership did not do what they were supposed to do. The Lord responds, though, saying to Moses and Aaron in Numbers 20:12, "And the LORD said to Moses and Aaron, "Because you did not believe in me, to uphold me as holy in the eyes of the people of Israel, therefore you shall not bring this assembly into the land that I have given them."

Moses recounts this experience beginning in Deuteronomy 3:23-27, "And I pleaded with the LORD at that time, saying, 'O Lord GOD, you have only begun to show your servant your greatness and your mighty hand. For what god is there in heaven or on earth who can do such works and mighty acts as yours? Please let me go over and see the good land beyond the Jordan, that good hill country and Lebanon.' But the LORD was angry with me because of you and would not listen to me. And the LORD said to me, 'Enough from you; do not speak to me of this matter again. Go up to the top of Pisgah and lift up your eyes westward and northward and southward and eastward, and look at it with your eyes, for you shall not go over this Jordan"

Do not think for a second that Moses said, "Well, okay God. No big deal, I am not going to get to go into the Promised Land." It was a big deal. He pleaded with the Lord to let him go in in the promised land. The man who the Lord communicated to face-to-face, a man who the Lord had revealed His glory to, a man who had been on his face with the Lord repeatedly, pleaded with the Lord. We see the outcome of that pleading in those verses from Deuteronomy:

"But the LORD was angry with me because of you and would not listen to me. And the LORD said to me, 'Enough from you; do not speak to me of this matter again. Go up to the top of Pisgah and lift up your eyes westward and northward and southward and eastward, and look at it with your eyes, for you shall not go over this Jordan."

We might think this is very harsh of the Lord – to not allow this man Moses to enter in – but Moses in this act was a man that allowed his anger to control his actions and robbed God of the glory He was due. Moses was a "type" of a greater one to come, yet Moses was but a man. The writer of Hebrews is going to remind us that there is one greater than Moses. While Moses was a great man, he was not a sinless man. Moses points us to the Savior, but Moses needed a Savior as do we all. Praise the Lord a "greater than Moses has come," and His name is Jesus!

Have you ever allowed your emotion or your anger to cause you to speak rashly with your lips? That is exactly what has happened now to Moses. Out of his anger, he commits this sin. What was Moses great sin?

First, he disobeyed the command of the Lord. This is the first thing that the Lord calls him out on in Numbers 20:12, "the Lord said to Moses and Aaron, 'Because you have not believed me.'" What was the sin? In his mind, I think Moses went back to Exodus 17 where he struck the rock, and it was a great demonstration. There, it was a drama being enacted – he struck the rock, and the water came. Now the Lord said, simply speak. That does not have the same effect, does it?

It is very easy for us to forget that the word of God is the power. It is not in the demonstration. It is not in the swinging of the of the rod or the strategy. It is the word of the Lord that brings the power. In the church today, we sometimes are just like Moses. Rather than listening and obeying the command of the Lord, we gravitate back to experience and pragmatism. Rather than listening to a fresh word from God, we do what we remember worked. God was telling him to speak to the rock this time. The instruction was very clear and nowhere did God say anything about striking the rock.

It was a sin of rebellion and disobedience. He did not trust that what God said to do would be sufficient. F.B. Meyer says, "It was a lack of faith that led Moses to strike the rock twice. He forgot that neither the rod nor the speech affected the results, but the power of God that brought it through the work through with him." In other words, it is not the method or the program or the strategy – it is the word of God. I believe that is how God builds his church. He builds his church through the power of His word.

Secondly, Moses misappropriated the gifts of God. It is interesting that the very rod – the gift that God had given to be with him since the burning bush as a symbol that God would use of His divine presence and power in his life – which had been a source of blessing, now becomes a source of judgment because he misappropriated the gifts of God. We must also be careful in the church today that we do not misappropriate the gifts that God has given to the church. The very thing that was once used for blessing was now a source of judgment in the life of this man.

Thirdly, Moses diminished the glory of the Lord. If you think for one minute what Moses did was not a big thing, listen to what the Lord says, "Because you have not believed me to treat me as holy in the sight of the sons of Israel." What is it that Moses did? Moses drew attention to him and Aaron rather than putting the attention upon God – where it belonged.

Moses comes out to the people with his spontaneous dialogue saying, "You rebels, must we fetch water out of this rock?" Who was getting the glory out of that? Moses and Aaron were usurping the glory that belonged to God. I would remind you that God does not share his glory with any other. In Isaiah 42:8 we read, "I am the Lord, that is my name, my glory, I give to no other." Isaiah 48:11 says, "For my sake and my own sake, I do it for how should my name be profaned my glory. I will not give to another."

Moses and Aaron took the attention and the glory that should have been given to God on that day. They diminished the glory of God, but I believe there is something else going on here. Perhaps the gravest sin in all of this was that they distorted the "foreshadow" and the "type" of Christ. Listen to what the Bible says in 1 Corinthians 10: 1-4:

"For I do not want you to be unaware, brothers, that our fathers were all under the cloud, and all passed through the sea, and all were baptized into Moses in the cloud and in the sea, and all ate the same spiritual food, and all drank the same spiritual drink. For they drank from the spiritual Rock that followed them, and the Rock was Christ."

Do you see what is happening? In the Old Testament, there are many "types" and "foreshadows" of the Lord Jesus Christ. In Exodus 17, the Rock was struck, and the life-giving water flowed. Jesus is also to be struck – but once. He was struck at Calvary – smitten upon the cross. What He suffered and endured on the cross was once and for all, and he is not to be continually struck. When the Lord said to Moses this time to "speak to the rock", it is because the rock had already been struck.

Thanks to Calvary, we do not need the Lord to be crucified afresh and anew repeatedly. I think that is one of the great flaws of the Roman Catholic Church and their mass – they see that as the perpetual crucifying of the Lord over and over again. They are striking the rock over and over and over again. The rock has been struck once, and life-giving water comes forth. Now, all we need to do is speak to the Rock. Cry out to the Rock, call out to the Rock, and life-giving water shall come forth. That rock in the wilderness is none other than the Lord Jesus Christ.

Matthew Henry says it like this, "Worst of all, Moses defaced a beautiful picture of Jesus's redemptive work through the rock, which provided water in the wilderness." F.B. Meyer says, "Moses was to speak to the rock, not Smite at the Rock of Ages, was smitten only once." Now, what do we need to do to find that life-giving water? What did Jesus tell that woman at the well? "If you had asked me, I would have given you living water."

Do you need that life-giving water? Speak to the Rock. Ask Jesus, and He will give to you this life-giving water – this everlasting life!

LOOK AND LIVE

Because of a snowstorm, a fifteen-year-old teenager's path to church was diverted down a side street. For shelter, he ducked into the Primitive Methodist Chapel on Artillery Street. An unknown substitute lay preacher stepped into the pulpit and read his text – Isaiah 45:22, "Look unto me, and be ye saved, all the ends of the earth; for I am God, and there is none else."

Charles Spurgeon's autobiography records his reaction:

"He had not much to say, thank God, for that compelled him to keep on repeating his text, and there was nothing needed – by me, at any rate except his text. Then, stopping, he pointed to where I was sitting under the gallery, and he said, 'That young man there looks very miserable' ...and he shouted, as I think only a Primitive Methodist can, 'Look! Look, young man! Look now!' ...Then I had this vision – not a vision to my eyes, but to my heart. I saw what a Savior Christ was....Now I can never tell you how it was, but I no sooner saw whom I was to believe than I also understood what it was to believe, and I did believe in one moment. And as the snow fell on my road home from the little house of prayer, I thought every snowflake talked with me and told of the pardon I had found, for I was white as the driven snow"

"Look and live." Can it really be that simple?

Numbers 21 records one of the strangest experiences in the Old Testament. It is an experience that Jesus Himself would use as an illustration of His own death on the cross in a conversation with Nicodemus. Our focus in this chapter is "look and live." Here are the words as recorded by Moses in Numbers 21:4-9:

"From Mount Hor they set out by the way to the Red Sea, to go around the land of Edom. And the people became impatient on the way. And the people spoke against God and against Moses, "Why have you brought us up out of Egypt to die in the wilderness? For there is no food and no water, and we loathe this worthless food." Then the LORD sent fiery serpents among the people, and they bit the people, so that many people of Israel died. And the people came to Moses and said, "We have sinned, for we have spoken against the LORD and against you. Pray to the LORD, that he take away the serpents from us." So Moses prayed for the people. And the LORD said to Moses, "Make a fiery serpent and set it on a pole, and everyone who is bitten, when he sees it, shall live." So Moses made a bronze serpent and set it on a pole. And if a serpent bit anyone, he would look at the bronze serpent and live."

As we look at this experience, be reminded that these were the people of God – people redeemed with a mighty hand and people God was in covenant with – yet they were a rebellious, complaining people. There are three conditions of the people that I would like to draw your attention to in this story:

First: "These were a very, very blessed people."

These are the people that God had taken as His own possession and pitched His tent in their midst. God was dwelling among them! How amazing is that? These people were the people that had experienced the blessing and the presence of the creator God in their very midst.

Even though they were a very blessed people, we find them in this chapter to be a very disobedient and ungrateful people. These are the people that God brought to the very doorway of the promised land where they refused to enter. They were living in disobedience. In America, we have been blessed abundantly – blessed by God in more ways than we could ever number. This nation has received the favor and the blessing of God throughout our history. God has blessed this nation to be able to send missionaries all over the world. God has used America greatly to give help and aid to the nations.

We have been a blessed people, but like the nation of Israel, we have forgotten the past blessings of God and are ungrateful and unthankful for all His benefits. America may claim to be a Christian nation, but the reality is that we have failed to keep His commandments. Jesus said, "If you love me, you will keep my commandments." America has sinned against God and disobeyed God in so many ways. When I think about the state of our nation and all that we are going through, my prayer is this might be used by God to bring a great spiritual awakening to our land and country.

When I think about the condition of America, I hear the words of the prophet Isaiah ringing in my ears. Listen to the voice of this ancient prophet in Isaiah 1:2-6, "Hear, O heavens, and give ear, O earth; for the LORD has spoken: "Children have I reared and brought up, but they have rebelled against me. The ox knows its owner, and the donkey its master's crib, but Israel does not know, my people do not understand." Ah, sinful nation, a people laden with iniquity, offspring of evildoers, children who deal corruptly! They have forsaken the LORD, they have despised the Holy One of Israel, they are utterly estranged. Why will you still be struck down? Why will you continue to rebel? The whole head is sick, and the whole heart faint. From the sole of the foot even to the head, there is no soundness in it, but bruises and sores and raw wounds; they are not pressed out or bound up or softened with oil."

That may have been written around 700 BC, but it sounds as though it could have been written this century. America has forgotten the God that nourished and sustained her. America has become a disobedient people.

Second: "These were discouraged people."

Numbers 21:4 states that they "became impatient because of the journey." The King James Version says, "they were much discouraged because of the way." These people had spent the last forty years marching around in circles. The way had been very difficult, but when we are living lives of disobedience, our lives will indeed be difficult. When we choose to live according to our will rather than God's will, the Bible says, "the way of a transgressor is hard."

Our life will be difficult when we are living in disobedience. There will be much adversity that comes against us when we are going around in circles. This reminds me of the story of the pilot who came on the intercom to announce that all the airplane's navigational systems had been lost. He relayed that they did not currently know where they were or where they were going. He came back on in few minutes and announced he had good news. The good news was that they were making great time!

Many times, life seems as though we are going around in circles. Let us not forget that God is the one who is charting our course, and the Lord is the one who has a plan and will for our life. Whenever you ever feel that your life is going in circles or that you are lost during this journey, you need to stop where you are – it is not a matter of making great time! Look up and cry out to the Lord, for the Lord will direct your path. The children of Israel were disobedient people, which caused them to be a discouraged and dissatisfied people.

Third: "These were a defiant people."

It is recorded in Numbers 21:5, "And the people spoke against God and against Moses, "Why have you brought us up out of Egypt to die in the wilderness? For there is no food and no water, and we loathe this worthless food." To be honest, we have heard this complaint from these people before. This is the same complaint that we heard from the generation before them. They are on the brink of entering into the promised land again, yet here we have the same old song being sung by the people.

They complained against the very God that blessed them with manna from heaven every day! The King James Version says, "their souls loathed this light bread." The contemporary English version says, "We can't stand this awful food." The ESV says "This worthless food."

Is it not amazing how the blessings and benefits of God are now being demeaned by his people as being worthless, awful, and miserable? When you are out of the will of God and not walking with the Lord, you will come to a place where you will even begin to despise the very gifts and blessings of God. Here, it says specifically that they spoke against God and against Moses. They had the audacity to speak against the very God that had redeemed them. They were crying out against the very one who was sustaining their life in the wilderness.

Finally: "These were a dying people."

Their sinful defiance and disobedience brought the judgment of God upon them as the Bible says in Numbers 21:6, "the Lord sent fiery serpents among the people. And they bit the people, so that many people of Israel died. For the past forty years, they had been marching around in circles in the wilderness until a whole generation – those who refused to enter into the promised land – died in the wilderness. Can you imagine how many funerals there were out in that desert wilderness?

Now, this new generation is not starting off very well, either. In the first three verses of Numbers 21, they experienced their first victory. You would think this would lead them to have an encouraged outlook and trust in the Lord. Instead, they quickly return to the sins of their fathers who rebelled against God. The judgment of God came as deadly serpents into their camp to bite them, and many people were dying.

When I read this, I must wonder if we are talking about ancient Israel or about our own modern world – people that are very disobedient to God and to God's commands, people that are discouraged in the way, people that are dissatisfied with the very things that God has provided, people on many occasions defiant against God, and people who literally shake their fist in the face of God. We, too, are living in the land of the dying. In fact, all humanity has been snake-bitten. It happened in Genesis 3, and because of that snake, all humanity is dying.

The good news is God has a cure for our dilemma.

He is a God who extends grace and mercy even to those that are rebelling against Him – even to those that were defiant and were speaking out against God and Moses. God is very gracious. God is very merciful, and He provides a cure for their dilemma. The cure is found in God's instruction to Moses and the people.

Numbers 21:7-9 says, "And the people came to Moses and said, "We have sinned, for we have spoken against the LORD and against you. Pray to the LORD, that he take away the serpents from us." So Moses prayed for the people. And the LORD said to Moses, "Make a fiery serpent and set it on a pole, and everyone who is bitten, when he sees it, shall live."

Only God could save them from this judgment and certain destruction. When you think about this cure, notice what the scripture teaches us. First, this cure coming from the Lord begins with repentance. The people came to Moses and confessed their sin. Repentance is the doorway to salvation. Unless we repent, we shall all likewise perish. These people were guilty before God and now they are acknowledging their sin.

Second, this cure that the Lord is providing required faith. Where is the faith, you ask? God gave the instructions to the people that looking to a serpent upon a pole would stop them from dying. Does that make any sense to you? Why in the world would looking at a bronze serpent on a pole cure a deadly snake bite? How could that be the remedy for their dilemma? I believe many people in the camp refused to look. They remained in their tent, and thought it was foolishness. Others were likely too stubborn to look. It took faith to go out and to look to this pole – taking a look of faith and being rewarded with a renewed chance at life.

Third, this cure from the Lord was available to all. God did not tell Moses to take a bronze serpent and hide it somewhere. God Instructed Moses to take that serpent and lift it up on a pole, put it up on a standard, and raise it up so that it is available to everyone in the camp. How wonderful to know that there was not a single Israelite who desired to look that was turned away! Everyone had opportunity for it was available to all. It was free to all is it did not cost anything to look and be cured. It was not "look, be cured, and then give this amount of an offering." It was simply "look and live."

When we think about this story, we need to remember that what we are reading is not just about an ancient people and a dilemma of a snake bite. What we are reading is a foreshadowing of the glorious gospel of our Lord and Savior, Jesus Christ. Remember how Jesus used this story to illustrate his own death when talking with Nicodemus in John 3:14-15? "And as Moses lifted up the serpent in the wilderness, so must the Son of Man be lifted up, that whoever believes in him may have eternal life."

Jesus goes back into the Old Testament – into the book of Numbers – and teaches Nicodemus that the story of Moses and the brazen serpent was an illustration of what the Son of Man was going to experience. The Son of Man was going to be lifted on a pole – we call it the old, rugged cross. Numbers 21 is simply a foreshadowing of what the Lord Jesus Christ was going to experience at Calvary.

The comparison is very clear. It is the cross of Christ that is our remedy for sin. Remember, all humanity has been snake-bitten. We are all sinners who have come short of the glory of God. It happened in Genesis 3 when Adam and Eve listen to the voice of the serpent and disobey God – plunging all humanity into sin. Because of that sin and act of disobedience, death came into our world. All the pain, suffering, and death in human history is a result of man's cosmic rebellion against the Creator. That is the reason why there is coronavirus, cancer, diabetes, and on and on – it can all be traced back to one man's rebellion against God in the garden.

How great to know that the grace of God has provided a remedy for our sin problem! That remedy for us is not looking upon a serpent on a pole but looking to a Savior upon a cross. I like what John Newton said late in his life, "Many things I have forgotten, but two things I know for sure. I am a great sinner and Jesus is a great Savior." I pray that I would be reminded all the days of my life that I am indeed a great sinner – but let me not forget also that Jesus is a great Savior! Will you "look and live?"

THE BLESSINGS OF GOD WILL NOT CHANGE

(This chapter is contributed by Zad Tomberlin – Pastor of Bethlehem Baptist Church in Madisonville, TN. Zad is married to his wife, Tory, and they have three children – Elly, Ty, and Gibby. Pastor Zad is a graduate of Toronto Baptist Seminary in Toronto, Canada.)

I can remember my daddy telling me, "there are a couple of things that are sure in life – death and taxes." I remember him saying that, and that is true – especially here in the United States. But that is not all that is sure and certain. God's promises are sure and certain. As we look into God's word, we find His promises are true and steadfast. God's promises will hold true. They will come to pass. You can take that to the bank.

In Numbers 22, we encounter the people of Israel camped out on the plains of Moab. They are on the fringe of the promised land – they are close. They are closing in on the great promised land that the Lord has assured them they would possess. Now, there has been many ups and downs along the way. There has been a great deal of rebellion, disobedience, and complaining. We are also good at that. It comes natural to us as a lost men and women.

The Lord has set His affection on the people of Israel and despite their rebellion and despite their complaining, God seeks to bless them. Why? Because God loves them. They have experienced a victory in chapter 21, and they are drawing close to the promised land. They have no knowledge that there is an enemy who is seeking their destruction. The king of Moab is seeking to curse them so that he can have victory over them and destroy them.

Here in Numbers 22-24, the Lord provides for us a clear demonstration of His faithful covenant love towards His chosen people. What we see in theses chapters is the fact that no enemy nation, no worker of divination, no soothsayer or false prophet can do anything to hinder the purposes of God. God's purposes cannot be thwarted. God has determined to bless His people and bless them He will. He has set his covenant love upon them and He will bless them despite their rebellion.

That is good news for you and me. Despite our rebellion and disobedience, God has set His affection upon us and He will keep His covenant to us. These chapters remind us that often we are just like these Israelites – unaware that the enemy stands ready to destroy us, yet God is fighting for us. In fact, most of the time we are totally unaware, yet God is for us.

The children of Israel were unaware that the king of Moab was plotting to kill them. Often, we are too hard-headed to see our own demise. God opened the eyes of a donkey – may He open our eyes to see as well. So, we are going to see a contrast of Israel's rebellion and God's faithfulness to his covenant promises. God intends to bless them, and the Lord reveals His blessing by using this false prophet by the name of Balaam.

The question for us is how does the Lord bless His people?

Think about the problem that Balak the king of Moab faced. The problem that he faced was a pretty big problem. I think we can all relate with how this is unbelieving king felt. He was afraid and arrested by an unwarranted fear. He was fearful of the people of Israel – fearful of them taking his land. He knew the reality of what had happened to the Amorites. God wiped them out for their rebellion and harshness towards the people of Israel, so he was scared.

Fear often leads us to make bad decisions or make a rash, quick decision instead of being patient and listening to the Word of the Lord. Have you ever allowed fear to drive you to a bad decision? Yeah, me too. Balak's fear was unwarranted because the Lord had told Moses to leave Moab alone in Deuteronomy 2:9, "And the LORD said to me, 'Do not harass Moab or contend with them in battle, for I will not give you any of their land for a possession, because I have given Ar to the people of Lot for a possession." Often our fears are unwarranted, and we fear because we do not know the promises of God or we fail to rest upon them.

The King of Moab knew he could not defeat the nation of Israel on the battlefield, so he sought to curse them. There was a belief system in the ancient days of blessing and curses, and there were diviners (prophets for hire if you will) who could pray blessings or curses upon people. So, Balak sends his messengers to Balaam to say, "we know who you bless will be blessed and who you curse will be cursed."

Balaam had a reputation for being a successful diviner, but as we will learn, God will not be manipulated or coerced into going against His Word. He will not break His covenant. He will not curse the people He has promised to bless. God cannot be bought by anyone or anything. With God, "He means what he says, and he says what he means." My dad used to tell me that as well.

The Lord blesses his people by his presence and his protection – even when they are not aware of it.

Numbers 22-24 paints the whole picture of the main point, which is God intends to bless his people. Balaam goes and declares the Word of the Lord – a word of blessing and not curse. We learn that God is the One in charge, not some false prophet seeking money. Numbers 23:19 is a foundational statement revealing the immutability and faithfulness of God, "God is not man, that he should lie, or a son of man, that he should change his mind. Has he said, and will he not do it? Or has he spoken, and will he not fulfill it? Therefore, Balaam replies in verse 20, "Behold, I received a command to bless: he has blessed, and I cannot revoke it."

For those who are in Christ, those that are under the new covenant, we have nothing to fear. No unseen enemy, no hidden foe shall harm us. We are safe in the arms of Christ our Lord. The Lord is with us and where the presence of the Lord is there is protection. Our lives are hidden in Christ, and the Spirit dwells within us. That is good news is the Lord means to bless us!

If you have never trusted in the person of Christ, if you have never repented of your sins and believed upon Jesus, please do so now. Without Christ, you are sitting under the wrath of God because of your sin. God is a just God, and He will punish you if you die in your sin. If you stand before God in your own righteousness, it will not be sufficient. You need the righteousness of Christ. Trust Him today.

Even a dumb donkey sees what the greedy prophet cannot.

Balaam is an interesting character, but nothing as interesting as the experience with the talking donkey. Balaam was a man with a divided allegiance. Balaam – as a worker of divination – wanted to use God to make money. Greed was at the heart this man's ministry. The New Testament writer Jude gives a warning concerning following Balaam's example, "Woe to them! For they walked in the way of Cain and abandoned themselves for the sake of gain to Balaam's error and perished in Korah's rebellion."

Divination is clearly forbidden by the Lord in Deuteronomy 18:9-12, "When you come into the land that the LORD your God is giving you, you shall not learn to follow the abominable practices of those nations. There shall not be found among you anyone who burns his son or his daughter as an offering, anyone who practices divination or tells fortunes or interprets omens, or a sorcerer or a charmer or a medium or a necromancer or one who inquires of the dead, for whoever does these things is an abomination to the LORD. And because of these abominations the LORD your God is driving them out before you."

Balaam seems to be trying to play both worlds here – all for a dollar. Any man with a divided allegiance has no allegiance at all. The illustration is clear (and humorous) as the dumb donkey could see what the seer could not. It is funny because it is a lesson on humility for someone who was supposed to be able to speak to the gods, to manipulate the gods, and to call down a curse or a blessing.

The great Seer, or prophet, was unable to see the angel of the Lord standing before him three times with a sword ready to pierce him. The irony is found in the words of Balaam to his donkey, "If I had a sword in my hand, I would have killed you by now." The sword, though, was in the hand of the angel of the Lord – meant for Balaam. His donkey saw what he could not.

God can use whoever he chooses to bless His people –
even a greedy false prophet such as Balaam.

God does what He determined to do – bless Israel. God
has determined to bless His people despite themselves, so
He blesses them with His presence, He blesses them with
His protection, and He blesses them with deliverance.

He has been doing this since Genesis 3:15 when he made
a promise that from the seed of the woman would come
One who would crush the head of the serpent. Our great
Deliverer has come, and His name is Jesus. God promised
a Redeemer – a coming Messiah – and God always fulfills
His promises. In the garden – after Adam and Eve sinned
against God – we see both justice and grace. Justice as
they were driven out of the garden and the death process
began, and grace in the promise of One who would
restore all that they had forfeited.

God has turned the curse into a blessing for you and me.
Why would He do so? Because of His great love. God loves
you, and He is motivated out of love. He did not have to,
but He chose to. This act of love is what would bring Him
glory. Grace is seen as God chooses to bless and redeem
a people who are unworthy and underserving.

All God's promises find their "yes and amen" in the Lord
Jesus Christ. God keeps His word – He is faithful to what
He says in the past, in the present, and in the future.
Nothing can stop His covenant. God is on a mission to
glorify Himself by sending a Redeemer who is a Prophet,
Priest, and King – who would rescue not just Jews but
Gentiles as well. Scripture is unfolding every day, all
around us. God is calling out a people from every nation,
tribe, and people group. Why? For His name's sake. To
bring glory to His name.

In Christ, God has reversed the curse. He has turned the curse into a blessing. He is in the process of doing this in our lives as well. There is nothing that God cannot turn for good. Remember the story of Joseph? The end of the story is marvelous, and Joseph's words bring us great comfort. Joseph said to the brothers that sold him into slavery, "You meant it for evil, but God meant it for good."

Praise the Lord! God is taking all the evil, all the suffering, all the pain and working them into the tapestry of our lives. Today may look like a frazzled, frayed mess, but when we get on the other side, we will see the beautiful design that God has worked. Keep trusting in Him!

TYING UP LOOSE ENDS

Closing and finishing – not what us pastors are good at, right? Usually, when the preacher says, "and in conclusion..." he goes on for another fifteen minutes at least. We get this from the Apostle Paul. If you have read any of his writings, he will say, "finally, brethren..." and then continue for three more chapters. So, it has been handed down from pastor to pastor over these many centuries.

We now bring our meditations on Numbers to a close, and I hope that it has reinforced the reality that we need a good understanding of the Old Testament to rightly interpret the New Testament. I hope that we are mindful of the fact that we find Jesus on the pages of the Book of Numbers – just as we encounter Him in the Gospel.

Not only do we encounter Jesus in "type" and "foreshadow," we also encounter ourselves in the text. We are much more like these complaining Israelites than we want to admit. We often struggle with the same temptations and weaknesses that they did. Unbelief, fear, and frustration are not found only in the ancient people of God, because the contemporary Christians are not much different.

I want to remind you of one of the main truths of the book of Numbers. There are several, but one of the main truths of the book of Numbers is: "The same Lord who redeems is the Lord who sustains and sanctifies." The very same God that brought them out of Egypt is the same God who will bring them into the promised land.

When thinking about the book of Numbers, perhaps Dr. J. Vernon McGee said it best. This book could be titled "Pilgrim's Progress." McGee wrote, "When you look at the book of Numbers, what you find is the walking, the wandering, the warring, the working, the witnessing and the worshiping of God's pilgrims. It is a handbook for all pilgrims navigating the wilderness road of this world."

That is exactly where we find ourselves – pilgrims in a wilderness. We are not in paradise. Have you noticed that we are in the wilderness? We are living between salvation brought through justification in Christ alone and our future glorious day of glorification. We have been saved from the penalty of sin, but one day we will be saved from the very presence of sin. Today, we live in a sin-cursed world, but through a process called "sanctification" we are being saved from the very power of sin.

John Bunyan's classic work called "Pilgrim's Progress" is written as an allegory. I hope that everyone has read it at some point in your Christian life – if not, I recommend you do. Bunyan writes about our present journey and says, "God's grace is the most incredible and insurmountable truth ever to be revealed to the human heart, which is why God has given us His Holy Spirit to superintend the process of more fully revealing the majesty of the work done on our behalf by our savior."

We are all like Christian (the main character in Pilgrim's Progress), and we need the grace of God. We need to recognize that God is indeed superintending the work of sanctification in our lives, so the majesty and the beauty and the glory of what Christ has accomplished for us on the cross can be revealed. This world needs to see that being revealed. God needs to be revealed through human "shoe leather" – the human activity through human conduit.

We need to be the bright light in this dark world, and it is through the work of sanctification that this is happening in the people of God. Now, it is a wonderful thing to know that the very God who redeems is also the God who sanctifies and the God who guarantees our glorification. I also believe that Matt Chandler was right when he wrote, "If there is no evidence of sanctification taking place in your life, what assurance do you have of glorification?"

In other words, if you do not presently see the work of God going on in your life, you may want to check to make sure that the hope of glorification is a reality. You may have a problem. You see all of those that He justifies, He indeed sanctifies – and all of those that He sanctifies, He will one day glorify. That is the good news of the gospel, and the very same Lord who delivers is the Lord who sustains His people and who sanctifies His people.

Sanctification is never an easy process. As we learned in Numbers, it is often easier to get the Israelites out of Egypt than to get Egypt out of the Israelites. I can identify with that, and I find the struggle to be very real. I find that it is very difficult to get the world out of my heart, and I think that is the process of sanctification.

Like the Israelites, we can also grow discontent with the provision of the Lord and desire something more flavorful to our tastebuds. God provided their needs but not all their wants. God fed them every day for forty years, but that seemed boring and bland. Rather than being grateful, they became discontent. The Bible even says that their shoes did not wear out. That is an amazing thing, but I am sure some of us probably would not be happy wearing the same shoes for forty years, either! They entered the promised land with the same shoes they left Egypt in because God was providing for them. God was taking care of their every need, but they were not satisfied. They were discontent.

Often, I look in the mirror and see these ancient people looking back at me – for many times, I grow discontent with the blessings of the Lord. Many times, I have cravings for things that are not spiritual and things that would not aid in my sanctification. I am very much like these Israelites.

Another of one of the main truths of the book of Numbers is: "These people were blessed with God's continual presence." Is it not amazing that despite all the complaining, grumbling, and rebelling, God never left them? If you flip through Numbers and highlight or underline every time they rebelled, grumbled, or complained, you would be marking nearly every page of the book!

The amazing thing about it all is that – despite these people living in continual rebellion and being unappreciative and ungrateful for all that God provided – God never once packed up his tent and left. God never once removed the cloud or the fire that was leading them every single day. Even amid their rebellion, God's presence was with them.

They could see the cloud, they could see the fire, and they could see the tabernacle in the middle of their community – all serving as visual reminders that God was with them. That is a wonderful thing and a glorious truth. Have you ever stood at the crossroads and wished for a cloud to lead you? Have you ever stood at the crossroads and asked God to send an arrow showing which way to go?

We have something far better than a cloud in the sky or a pillar of fire. We have something far better than a tent or a tabernacle in the middle of our community. What do we have? We have the indwelling presence of the Holy Spirit. As born-again followers of Christ, we have been indwelt by the power of the Holy Spirit. Greater is He that is in you than he that is in the world. God within us is better than a tabernacle among us!

I think this is what Jesus talks about in the Upper Room, and I am glad that we have all four gospels for passages like these. There are some things in the Gospel of John that we cannot find anywhere else, and the Upper Room discourse is so full and rich. It contains the words of our Savior hours before going to the cross. He gathers that little band of disciples in the Upper Room, and he expounds for them great truths about the Holy Spirit.

Jesus says in John 14:16-18, "And I will ask the Father, and he will give you another Helper, to be with you forever, even the Spirit of truth, whom the world cannot receive, because it neither sees him nor knows him. You know him, for he dwells with you and will be in you. I will not leave you as orphans; I will come to you."

I love this phrase and the way it is translated in the modern translations. "I will not leave you as orphans. I will come to you." Is that not glorious? God dwells in the life of the believer.

Then Jesus says in John 14:26-27, "But the Helper, the Holy Spirit, whom the Father will send in my name, he will teach you all things and bring to your remembrance all that I have said to you. Peace I leave with you; my peace I give to you. Not as the world gives do I give to you. Let not your hearts be troubled, neither let them be afraid."

I cannot think of a better place to end our study! God is with us! He will never leave us – no matter how much we may act like spoiled children. He will finish what He began. The God that saves is the God who sanctifies – and one day will bring about our glorification. He guarantees that we will one day enter into our "promised land!"

Made in the USA
Columbia, SC
14 October 2023

24044779R10098